Contents

Introduction

Feng Shui is the ancient Chinese art of arranging everything around us to enable us to live in greater harmony with our environment. The characters that translate into the words Feng Shui, which are pronounced *fung shoy* or even *foong showay* (but with a short o), mean wind and water. This meaning derives almost from prehistory when the strongest forces of nature were indeed wind and water. The 'feng' can be likened to a stream of energy passing overhead just like a wind, and the 'shui' is water in the earth. Feng Shui effectively manipulates the energies or chi to help achieve a balance between man and his environment. There are many aspects of Feng Shui which are beyond the immediate scope or interest of the individual, such as its application to the layout of a city. However, a lot of it can be applied practically, and to great effect, in the home, office and garden.

The history of Feng Shui

It seems that Feng Shui goes back several thousand years. It was certainly practised in China 3000 years ago but may go back 5000 years or more. In China it was almost enshrined officially as the science of the state. Hum Yue was the ancient term for Feng Shui – Hum meaning, basically, heavenly path and Yue the earthly path, both referring to the energies of chi. The principles of the subject and the way it is practised are contained in some ancient texts such as *The Book of Songs* (*Shih Ching*) which was written over many years commencing in the ninth century BC. Significant development occurred in the Han dynasty, from 206 BC to 224 AD, with the resulting compilation of the *Book* or *Record of Rites* (*Li Chi*) by Kuo Po. Kuo Po applied Feng Shui to the positioning of graves and in the later Sung dynasty (960 to 1279 AD) Wang Chi applied it to house building.

To some, the one figure who was responsible for Feng Shui and its development to the point it has reached today was Yuen Kuen Chok who studied the art during the Tang dynasty (618 to 906 AD). He wrote much on the subject and laid the base of the practice as it is used today. There are also more recent published works such as the *Imperial Encyclopaedia* (*Ku Chin T'u Shu Chi Ch'eng*) of the eighteenth century. In China, Feng Shui was and is practised a great deal, save only for a comparatively brief and enforced break during the era of the Cultural Revolution.

The west has been relatively slow in taking up the philosophies and practice of Feng Shui. It was not until the late nineteenth century that some appreciation of the technique reached westerners, in the main through the visits and travels of missionaries.

Different approaches to Feng Shui

There are several schools or approaches to Feng Shui that essentially are due to their place of origination. The first, the Form School, was developed by scholars who inhabited a region of China dominated by hills that provided a dramatic backdrop with impressive peaks and troughs. This approach dwelt upon the characteristics of the scenery and its different formations.

A little later, and in a different area of China and with a very different landscape of flat plains, scholars applied Feng Shui in an area where there were no such mountains and hills. The scenery was plain and bland and an altogether different approach had to be adopted. This led to a scheme based upon the points of the compass and so the Compass School was formed (sometimes also called the Fukien method). Many practitioners of Feng Shui now use a combination of these two working practices.

A third system has been used by some, although its basis is very much more tenuous than the other methods. It comprises a blend of sayings and folklore, observations and fabricated practices but nevertheless has been developed and used by some.

The scope of Feng Shui

Feng Shui is an all-encompassing approach to living and to ordering one's environment. It combines what at first seems a curious mix of factors:

- philosophy
- interior (and exterior) design
- divination
- plain common sense
- (and in some cases) astrology

For many people it is the 'oracle' that should be consulted before many decisions are taken, and in China it often is the focus around which people live and how they plan their homes and lay them out internally. It can be used to choose the most opportune days upon which to start something, whether it be a marriage, building a new home, commencing a new business or starting a new job. It can even be used to decide the location of a relative's grave. It thus forms a predictive tool for life's situations whether impending changes involve the individual, their family or their finances.

The Basics of Feng Shui

One of the important components of Feng Shui is the theory of the five elements, which is considered later in this section. Other factors to be explained are yin and yang, chi and the concept of trigrams. Practitioners of Feng Shui regard their surroundings as an expression of chi and it is therefore appropriate to consider first the topic of chi, and Tao (pronounced, cow) with which it is inextricably linked and from which Feng Shui is derived.

Tao

Early western proponents of Feng Shui found that Taoism was a religion and philosophical system well established in China. Taoism, otherwise known as *the way* (or the other way), existed along the established ideals of Confucianism and in some respects offered an alternative. The philosophy of Taoism was developed several hundred years ago from old traditions of foretelling and the worship of nature (one can readily see from this a clear link with Feng Shui). Scholars of the time include Laotzu who wrote the *Tao-te-Ching* and Chuang-tzu to whom was attributed the *Chuang-tzu*. These philosophers helped to formulate the concept of Dao (or Tao) for the way, or path and the source of all creation. Not only that, Dao was considered to be the hidden impetus behind the enormously diverse happenings in the natural world. Followers based their spiritual life upon a combination of Dao and nature because they saw in nature a permanent and harmonious system creating a stable social order, far superior to that imposed by man and the powers of the state. Although Taoism can thus be seen to be fundamental, it is quite different from the God of other religions.

Followers and teachers of Taoism therefore

conformed to this natural order of things and showed great interest in issues relating to health including herbal medicine and good diet. The individual is meant to fall into line with the way the universe works, the Tao, and, through following this path, ultimately accomplishes unity with the Tao. A further development of Tao was that its followers sought long life, if not immortality, through the use of magic and alchemy. While immortality can hardly be achieved, an overall system of hygiene was developed which is still used and which emphasises the need for regular breathing and concentration to confer long life and help prevent disease.

In the past, many Chinese would temporarily leave the bustle and pressures of life and return to nature, either in the countryside or at a mountain retreat. This allowed them to rest and be healed, and during this time they might paint, write poetry or perhaps compose music in an attempt to encapsulate the positive forces at the heart of nature itself. This practice also instilled in the Chinese a very positive approach to life itself, and an assertion of their health, wellbeing and vitality.

Some Taoists did indeed seek immortality through the use of herbs or chemicals, or even through the location of the 'isles of the immortals'. However, the majority were more often interested in the benefits of herbal medicine and pharmacology and it seems that they did much to advance these subjects. In addition they developed good diets and gymnastic and massage routines to help maintain the body's condition.

It can be seen quite readily that the principal aims of Feng Shui, arranging everything around us to generate greater harmony with the environment, do have much in common with the practice of Tao.

Chi

Chi, pronounced 'chee' and often spelled ch'i, is thought by the Chinese to be the most important aspect of Feng Shui. Chi encompasses everything and holds together all the different aspects and factors involved in Feng Shui. It is the energy and force that flows all around and within and accordingly is sometimes called the cosmic breath. Chi is basically the life force, giving life to everything whether it be the movement of the stars, the weather and the changing seasons or the spiritual and physical changes within ourselves. Chi cannot be seen, heard or felt; it does not register upon any of our senses. It is apparent merely by its effect. In essence it refers to beneficial currents, whether generated by a propitious environment or created by a well-ordered room with freely-flowing air.

A house situated on a particular site in a certain way will be subject to highly positive and beneficial chi (which itself creates a healthy environment) and, by generating a positive environment within the home, can also help to produce a prosperous life. The aim is to have the chi entering the site, and, after moving around gently, to have it leave at the other side. Within the house the chi should be allowed and encouraged to move in different ways, sometimes being slowed down, on other occasions being speeded up. In a room where there is a lot happening, such as a general living room, the chi can be strengthened by reflection between mirrors. While in a room which is quieter, such as a bedroom or sitting room, it needs to be directed around the room in a peaceful way. The chi also needs an exit from the room which should be different from the access, so a room with just one door cannot allow chi to circulate and it will become a stagnant area.

Feng Shui is basically the arrangement of our immediate environment to enable us to benefit from the good effects of chi. Experts in the discipline of Feng Shui regard our surroundings as a representation and manifestation of chi. There are three conditions or stages of chi – sheng chi, si chi and sha chi.

Sheng chi

Sheng chi means moving upward and is a positive type of chi to be found in places that are bright, refreshing and uplifting. By extrapolation, people in these places are generally content and happy. Sheng chi is to be found by a wood, the sea, a park, a field or other naturally pleasant setting. When an individual possesses sheng chi, they are full of hope and optimism. When the moon is near to its full phase, it is called sheng.

Si chi

Si chi is the opposite of sheng chi – reducing, lessening or dying and has an overall negative impact. A location that is disorderly and decayed has si chi and in the environment around us si chi is reflected in sick animals, exhausted soil and therefore very poor vegetation. It is not surprising then that people are affected in a similar way, being sick, poorly and depressed. When the moon is almost new, it is said to be si.

Sha chi

Sha chi is a little different from sheng chi and si chi. It is harmful energy. The chi that is possessed when people are angry or when a place has a threatening or peculiar feel to it. Sha chi originates from negative surroundings both above and below ground and depending upon its origin can cause detrimental effects. Sha chi from below the ground causes sickness and saps energy and so a person may feel tired and apprehensive for no obvious reason. This would certainly apply to a house built in such a place, for example in a low, dank and possibly dark location. Beneficial chi is generally considered to move around in a gentle way, following a curving path, but sha chi travels in straight lines.

Sha chi emanating from above ground causes nervous complaints and illnesses. It may result in troubles in someone's personal life (such as broken relationships) and financial concerns whether personal or relating to business. Sha chi can affect houses in a number of ways, some of

Figure 1 – Sha chi will adversely affect houses sited in these positions

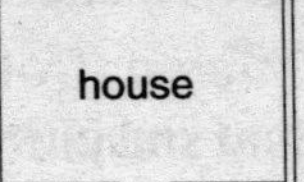

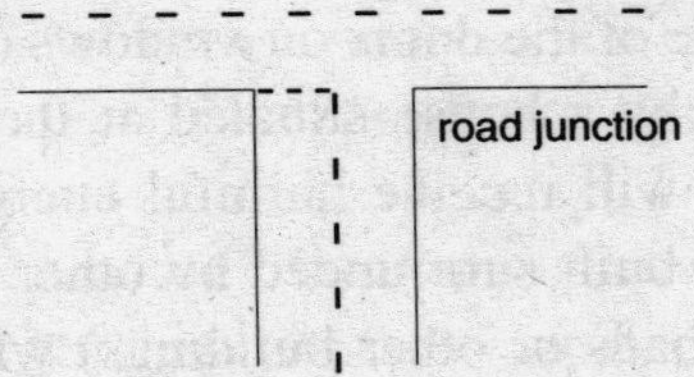

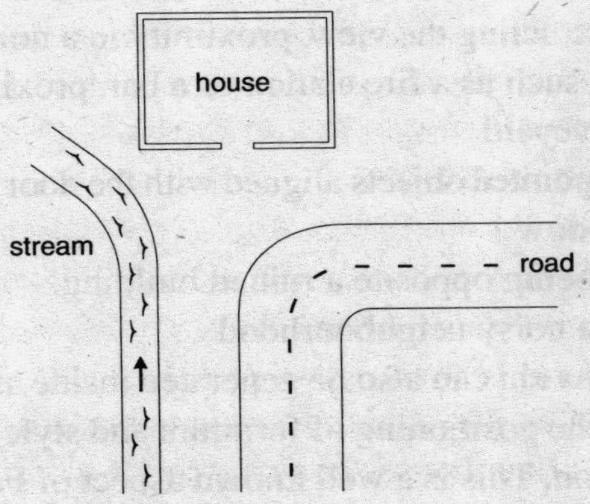

which will be mentioned later but here are some examples.

It is well known that sha chi will affect a house detrimentally if the house is sited at a T-junction in the road or if a road or a river runs straight at or from one of the doors or windows (*see* figure 1). Similarly, a house situated at the end of a cul-de-sac will receive harmful energy as will one that is built surrounded by other structures (bridges, roads or other buildings) which completely box it in. Other configurations that can create sha chi include: overhead cables or wires obstructing the view, proximity to a noisy building such as a fire station or a bar, proximity to a graveyard

- pointed objects aligned with the door or a window
- being opposite a ruined building
- a noisy neighbourhood

Sha chi can also be generated inside a building by the positioning of furniture and style of decoration. This is a well known aspect of Feng Shui and is encountered in several instances later in the book. Let us consider these factors a little more.

Generation of sha chi

When a building is faced by the corner of another building, perhaps across the road, it will be subject to sha chi. This sha chi is often referred to as 'secret arrows' in which the arrow flies from the offending building, threatening the building or site in question. The effects can be varied but may include the occupants being particularly prone to illnesses. Whenever there is a building by a road or some other public way, the edge of that building will produce sha chi which may be directed at your house.

The actual site upon which a house is built may also contribute to the sha chi. Within the ground itself, faults and similar features create sha chi. This may also include small valleys which if straight will generate sha chi. External, man-made features such as poles and wires, used for various reasons including the provision of the utilities, can also be detrimental because they carry the sha chi. Wires should preferably run at a low angle to the building, almost parallel to it, and poles, posts and trees should not be positioned immediately outside windows.

As will be discussed later, there are many configurations inside the house that should either be avoided or amended, to avoid or lessen the sha chi. For this reason, stairs should not descend immediately facing the outer door, and the back door of a house should not be visible when entering through the front door. In both cases good chi is allowed to flow directly out of the house before it has been able to circulate. It is also better to avoid a layout in which the house is split by a corridor at the centre. This may lead to a division of the house, which is a bad thing, but the corridor may encourage the chi to move too rapidly.

This brings us to the next factor involved in Feng Shui, which is to be considered before looking at the application of Feng Shui. In the flow of chi, there are negative and positive aspects, known as yin and yang, the subject of the next section.

Yin and Yang

Yin and yang are the be all and end all: the cause of life and death. The Chinese equate the earth, or creation with yin and the sky or heaven with yang. Pictorially, yin is represented by a line of two dashes while yang is a continuous line, each derived from the square and circle which in turn

Figure 2

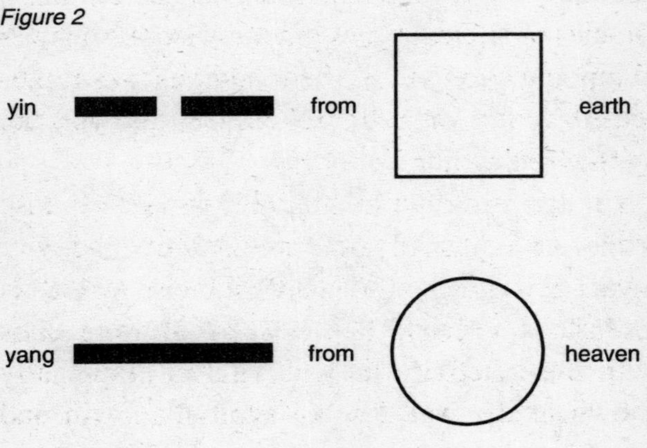

Figure 3 – the symbol for yin and yang

represent the earth and heaven, respectively (*see* figure 2). The origin of this lies with the fact that yin and yang lines were used as ancient oracles. Oracles of ancient times gave a yes or no answer to any question put to them and yes was represented by the yang, unbroken, line and yin, no, by the broken line.

Yin and yang are inextricably linked because while yin is restful and yang is active, activity invariably ends with rest and likewise rest leads to further activity. The activity of yang ends with the inactivity of yin. This is graphically shown in the well known symbol for yin and yang which is often called the T'ai ch'i, something quite different from the system of exercise for which the full name is T'ai chi chu'an (*see* figure 3).

Although yin and yang are effectively opposites, together they produce a balance and within each there is some part of the other, represented in the symbol by the dot of contrasting colour – white in black and black in white. Yin and yang and their negative/positive aspects also relate to the individual, the home and his or her occupation. A number of characteristics or properties can be attributed to yin or yang and in turn the physical makeup of a person will be one or the other. The table opposite shows some typical properties.

The manifestation of yin and yang in the person

When applied to the personality, yin is gentle, quiet and magnetic while yang is fiery, active

Yin	Yang
Earth	Sky
Creation	Heaven
Matter	Spirit
Winter	Summer
Dark	Bright
Cold	Warm
Night	Day
Water	Fire
Down	Up
North	South
Female	Male
Inner	Outer
Indoors	Outdoors
Passive	Active
Negative	Positive
Receptive	Creative

and intense. At birth, everyone is either yin or yang in their physical constitution. It is sometimes possible to determine which one you are by studying the features of your face with the aid of a mirror.

Physical features

The yin person has features that tend to be well-spaced and set apart from an imaginary line that bisects the head from chin to forehead. Thus their features may include a cleft at the end of the nose, a gap in the front teeth, eyes well set apart, a large mouth with full lips. Mild climates tend to generate this type of character.

Not unexpectedly, the yang person has facial features which tend to be concentrated nearer to the imaginary centreline. The eyes tend therefore to be closer set, the nose small and flat and the lower jaw is square set. This type of person is thought to come from climatic extremes, including the cold and mountainous areas.

Attributes

Each type of person can be related to the various attributes and therefore a yin person tends to reveal him or herself through thoughts and a typical occupation would be teaching, writing or research. The yang person uses actions to express him or herself and typical occupations would be sport, business, engineering and the armed services. However, it is perhaps obvious that a yin type may have a yang occupation and vice versa.

When a person considers what will be the ideal surroundings for them, it is necessary to accommodate the physical constitution and the occupation. For the former, a complementary environment is required and that means the opposite is needed; a yang person will need a predominantly yin milieu. The opposite then applies for a yin person. The surroundings should also be made to match your job so that if your occupation is yin, there should be a yin area to promote thought. These varying factors can be summarised as follows:

Physical Constitution	Occupation	Nature of Surroundings	Special area required
yin	yin	mainly yang	yin
yin	yang	almost exclusively yang	
yang	yang	mainly yin	yang
yang	yin	almost exclusively yin	

This type of analysis provides a quick guideline for arranging our individual environment. This theme will be developed in later sections.

The five elements

As already mentioned, the five elements are another important aspect of chi and therefore Feng Shui. The five elements are wood, metal, fire, water and earth. Many different oriental philosophies and medical practices are based upon the essential structure of the five elements. Each element confers certain characteristics upon the nature and personality of the individual and, in addition, there are typical associations when it comes to attitudes, occupations, likes and dislikes. It is actually considered beneficial to have some of each element in your overall personality as this confers a balance to the individual and it is useful when it comes to the application of Feng Shui. These elements are not related in any way to the astrology studied and practised in the west; they are essentially all part of the makeup of the character of an individual.

Individuals are considered to have some part of each element in their makeup, but the particular characteristics of one element are shown more strongly than the others and dominate the overall disposition. Each element is now considered with its dominant characteristics and associations and it may be possible to recognise in yourself the dominant element of your makeup.

Wood

Otherwise known as *Mu*, the pioneer, wood brings its natural properties to the individual. It is strong, often pliable and can take a lot of strain. It has roots which usually go very deep into the ground providing sustenance and stability. In addition it produces leaves, flowers and possibly fruit that are, of course, seeds that are spread for the perpetuation of the species.

Rectangular, upright shapes are associated with wood, whether it be tall buildings or steep-sided hills. Interior design corresponding to this element would be of an essentially rectangular pattern. Green and blue is the colour associated with this element, apart from dark blues which fit elsewhere. Spring is the season of wood and anyone born in this season (roughly from the beginning of February to the beginning of May) is optimistic and bursting with ideas. Some of the other aspects of character corresponding to this element are given opposite.

Illness may result from imbalances and in the case of this element, typical complaints would include pains in the back, irritability, indecision, liver and gall bladder ailments, weakness or

Wood	
Positive Attributes	*Negative Attributes*
active	anger
practical	(should avoid wind)
likes to win	
can be domineering	
demonstrative	
busy	
kind and friendly	
generous	
romantic	
good co-ordinator	

paralysis of the limbs, and eye problems. These reflect the parts of the body that tend to be linked with wood and hence the areas that suffer when there is a disparity.

Certain occupations are allied more with wood than the other elements. These include many of the creative vocations such as writing, painting, photography, music and interior design. These professions clearly exemplify the creative nature of such individuals. In addition, occupations relating to architecture and the landscape would not be uncommon.

In the home it is important that there is a quiet corner for contemplation and creation, whether it be composing music, drawing, painting or simply reading.

Metal

Metal is the catalyst, *Chin*, and is considered to strengthen. It is also very workable and versatile and is used in a whole host of objects for both everyday, functional use from vehicles and machines to wire and computers and in items of great beauty such as jewellery.

The shapes associated with metal are the round and the oval which are reflected in the land by way of rounded hills and in buildings through the use of domes and similar structures. Interior themes comprise regular, rounded shapes and patterns and the colours of metal are typically white, grey, silver or similar. Autumn is the season corresponding with metal and those born in the period from early August to early November could well be the type who want everything just so – perfectionists. In addition to liking order and justice, other attributes are:

Metal

Positive Attributes	*Negative Attributes*
organised	inflexible
severe	sorrow
likes to control	(should avoid dryness)
exact	
appreciates quality	
moral	
wants to be right	

Diseases of the large intestine and lungs and other conditions relating to the spine and also depression are possible results of an imbalance of metal.

The attributes of metal that relate, among

others, to order and organisation find a suitable outlet in occupations such as the police or armed forces, the arts, the legal profession, computing and certain branches of engineering. The home should be tidy and well organised with a corner set aside for contemplative thought.

Fire

Known as the magician, *Huo*, fire is obviously full of life and brightness and is hot and dry. Hot deserts naturally fall under its control.

The fundamental shape of fire is considered to be an elongated triangle which is reflected in nature by jagged, pointed hills and mountains and in man-made features by pointed spires and roofs. Designs inside buildings would incorporate bright, cheery patterns possibly with a radiating theme. As would be expected, the colours associated with this element include all shades of red and also purple. The colour red is thought to be very propitious be it only red bricks, or red paving stones in a path. Summer is the season associated with fire and anyone born between early May and early August will be full of vitality. Other characteristics of this element include:

Fire

Positive Attributes	*Negative Attributes*
courageous	rashness
perceptive	impulsiveness
courteous	(should avoid heat)
charitable	
communicative	
likes excitement	
loving	
dislikes boredom	

There are many conditions and illnesses that can result from a disproportion of fire. Heart disease, circulatory problems (such as high blood pressure), muscular and digestive complaints are all likely, as is emotional upset and similar ailments where the origin lies with matters of the heart.

Occupations that readily match individuals covered by this element include any profession in which fire is involved and also those of a mathematical or numerical nature (accounting, for example) and those involving modern technology, such as computing and electronics. The home of such people should ideally be, and it is often the case, a warm welcoming environment suitable for receiving visitors but also for private moments which are greatly treasured.

Water

Known as the philosopher, *Shui*, water is the element that cleanses and rejuvenates – the very source of life. Flowing water follows its course naturally till it finds its way to the ocean. All areas where water is found, by seas, rivers and also by man-made waterways are influenced by this element.

The colours associated with water are dark shades – black, navy blue and similar. The wave form is the basic shape associated with water and this becomes undulating, rolling countryside on land. Internal themes follow this shape with flowing designs and surfaces. Winter is the time of year linked with water and anyone born between early November and early February will have a very emotional aspect to their character but will quite often cover up their feelings. Other characteristics of this element are shown in the table below.

Water

Positive Attributes	*Negative Attributes*
honest	fear
imaginative	can be secretive
wise	(should avoid cold)
ambitious	
independent	
innovative	
intelligent	

Illnesses due to a imbalance of water include nervous problems such as phobias, depression and lethargy; circulatory conditions such as low or high blood pressure; arthritis and other diseases of the joints and certain digestive ailments.

Professions that can be linked to water, in addition to anywhere water is used, are those which incorporate transport and commerce in general or involve communication. Furthermore, a number of complementary medical therapies and working with pharmaceuticals also correspond to water. In the home, the emotional aspects of the character of the individual should be matched by a place that can easily be made private and quiet.

Earth

As will be shown later, earth, the diplomat, *T'u*, is in a way central to everything else as it is the element that holds all the other elements. In its simplest form it is the ground or soil that not only enables life to grow but also takes back the dead organisms and recycles them into new life. It represents a complete balance.

Not surprisingly, the colours connected with

earth are browns, yellows and oranges and the fundamental shape is essentially a planar surface i.e. flat land with broad buildings with square elevations. Unlike the other elements, there is no particular time of year that is strongly linked with earth. However, it is sometimes associated with the summer, at the end of the season for fire, around early August. Those born at this time tend to be kind-hearted and caring and helpful towards others. Further characteristics associated with this element include:

Earth

Positive Attributes	*Negative Attributes*
honest	worry
patient	can be stubborn
gregarious	(should avoid damp)
loyal	
sympathetic	
compassionate	
punctilious	
likes to be needed	

Typical ailments connected with an imbalance of earth affect primarily the stomach and pancreas, and create certain nervous disorders. These include digestive problems which may involve conditions such as anorexia, diabetes, anxiety, insecurity and confusion.

Occupations that match individuals under this element include charitable work and health care. The various aspects of construction (foundations, tunnelling, building in general) in which there is a very close involvement with the ground are also appropriate as are the financial service sectors of banking, investments and related activities. The home revolves around providing comfort, whether it is in the kitchen, dining room or lounge.

Implications of the five elements

Identifying your own element and that of your partner and children can lead to a greater understanding of personal relationships and may help to avoid or resolve domestic difficulties that arise. It can also be useful when choosing and setting out a home.

It has to be appreciated that each of the five elements relates to the others and has a certain interaction with them. Some practitioners of Feng Shui call this the three cycles; these are the cycles of generation, destruction and mitigation (or moderation). The cycles are presented in simple terms below:

Generation cycle	**Destruction cycle**
earth supports metal	earth absorbs water
metal contains water	water extinguishes fire
water supplies wood	fire melts metal
wood feeds fire	metal cuts wood
fire helps earth	wood hinders earth

These inter-relationships can be represented graphically and by doing so the cycle of mitigation or moderation becomes clear (*see* figure 4). This means that one of the elements has a moderating

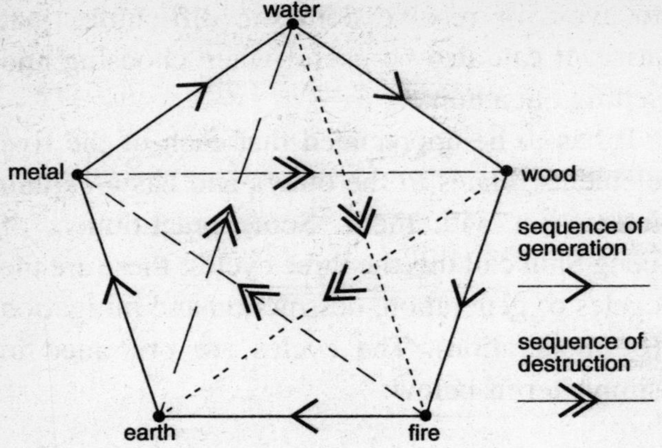

Figure 4 – the sequences of generation and destruction

influence on two others that are interacting. For example, and consulting the diagram, it can be seen that wood moderates the interaction between water and fire. In each case, the moderator lies between the two elements that are conflicting. In summary:

Moderation cycle
wood moderates between water and fire

fire moderates between wood and earth
earth moderates between fire and metal
metal moderates between earth and water
water moderates between metal and wood

The relevance of these interactions and the benefit of appreciating them comes to the fore later in our study when the element for an individual can be matched with compass directions (and their appropriate elements) to select suitable colours etc. to create the most harmonious situation possible.

Significance of the five elements

Each of the five elements is shown in the landscape by particular features or shapes of land forms and in the environment created by man, through the various shapes of buildings. Referring back to the personal attributes and characteristics listed previously and linking this to the properties and features described in this section allows, amongst other things, guidance to be drawn on the suitability of buildings for professions. In each case, the aspects that each element symbolises forms the basis for the analysis. Thus, for example, wood is shown in the earlier analysis to represent creativity, lots of ideas and to be associated with professions that utilise these qualities (*see* The Five Elements – Wood). This picture is reinforced by the details given below:

Wood

This is represented by structures that resemble the upright shape of trees. So in the natural landscape, high, steep-sided hills (but not with pointed peaks) fall into this group. Within the built environment, one naturally thinks of skyscrapers, blocks of flats, large factory chimneys and similar features. Such shapes are in the main of recent origin, reflecting more modern techniques of construction. However, a building that does not necessarily comply with the wood shape but is constructed out of wood, could fall within this category.

Buildings falling within the scope of this element are taken to be associated with creation and growth. This means that professions and businesses such as those in the care sector, catering, the creative areas such as artists and designers of whatever type, would ideally be housed in buildings within this element. Perhaps the most obvious occupation to pursue in a 'wood building' would be the manufacture of wooden items, be they pieces of furniture or handmade toys.

Metal

Metal is taken to be reflected in rounded features which in the landscape is rounded, dome-shaped hills and in buildings, anything with a domed appearance, a feature that is becoming more prevalent in some sectors of modern architecture, as well as being found in the architecture of the past. Arches and circular features would also be included in this category, and in the main, buildings with such features tend to be rather special: large buildings intended for the gathering of many people, or for ceremonies whether state or civic.

Buildings with this sort of structure are ideal for ventures and businesses of a financial nature as metal has a natural association with money. In addition, manufacturing with metal, and the sale of items associated with metal (such as jewellery) are readily included in this element. However, because metal is also the material from which weapons are made, it can represent aggression, in business for example. In this case it is important that the surroundings belong to a complementary element.

Fire

The flames within a fire are usually represented as flickering, stretched out, triangular shapes with points. Thus in the natural environment, fire is shown in pointed mountain tops although it need not necessarily just be found on mountains. Buildings that reflect this shape clearly include churches and temples that have steep spires, towers or similar features. There are also many other buildings with towers or steep roofs that can be taken to represent fire. Indeed, many domestic houses have roofs with quite a steep pitch which may be taken to represent fire. Any connection with learning, such as schools and libraries, would benefit from a building with a fire shape in some aspect of its design.

Water

Water is rather different from the other elements because its shape is determined by the shape of the container in which it is held. However, it is generally accepted that it possesses a curved if irregular form which in the landscape is represented by hills that roll gently and are without any definite trend in their shape, that is, they do not form a chain or a definite circular shape. When it comes to buildings, this category may be more difficult to qualify. In some respects it can end up as the miscellaneous of all the elements, because buildings with strange or complex shapes are included, although they should have a soft, rounded outline. A lot of modern architecture uses vast expanses of glass in buildings and this is also taken to represent water. However, it is preferable that the glass be used with wood and/or metal as they are part of the sequence of generation outlined in figure 4.

Looking back to the characteristics associated with this element, we can see intelligence, innovation, imagination and ambition which, with a natural tendency for communication, points clearly to the performing arts for buildings within this element. In addition, other suitable professions include the media and computing.

Earth

By comparison with hills and mountains, the earth is relatively flat and so features such as plains and plateaux are included. Low hills that maintain a flat profile would also be considered as a feature of this element, as would some mountains with extensive flat summits. When considering buildings, this element is obviously represented by those with flat roofs of which there are many examples – office blocks, apartments and so on. In addition, because an enormous number of buildings are made, in part or whole, with bricks and/or concrete, they will show some qualities of the earth element even if other features suggest an influence from another element. In addition to the construction activities mentioned earlier (*see* The Five Elements – Earth) farming has a natural association with this element.

Matching buildings with locations

Each of these five elements has a significance in two ways. Firstly the building may belong to a particular element and then the building may be situated in a location that has the same or a different elemental association. The implications for each type of building (i.e. each element) are now considered briefly within the five different locations available (wood, fire, etc).

Wood

Bear in mind the typical immediate environment of this element, whether urban or rural. A building within the element wood will clearly be well suited to a wood environment; the latter may be other wooden buildings, trees or tall tree-like buildings. This is a good and reliable set up. When the wood building is in a location that is essentially metal in its characteristics, there is the potential for conflict and ill-fortune. From the sequence of destruction (*see* figure 4) we can see that metal destroys wood so a wood building in metal surroundings is likely to have a negative influence on the resident business and/or people. This may show in physical injury or commercial problems – in effect the building would end up giving to the surroundings. The converse is true of a wood building in a fire location. Fire is fed by wood, in other words the occupation carried out in the building would have a net loss, although not in a negative way. Buildings which naturally house a function that gives something to an area include hospitals. As with the wood/metal combination, this would not be such a good location for a business due to the net loss which would be experienced.

The combination of a wood-element building in a water-element location is very good because water is linked to wood in the sequence of generation (*see* figure 4). This means that the one feeds the other and the implication is that whatever activity is housed in the building, it will flourish. When situated in an earth-element location, a wood building has the potential to be quite productive. The earth feeds the wood, but can only do so for a limited time so it would be necessary to compensate for this in some way.

Metal

Because of the specific characteristics (domes,

arches, etc.) of the form of the building in the metal element, it is not the natural choice for many people when considering what type of building to erect. A metal-element building in a metal-element location is consequently not particularly common. If it does occur, the activity carried out within the building should not conflict with the general activities of the area. Metal destroys wood, thus a metal-element building in a wood-element location could dominate the surroundings leading not only to financial success but even to exploitation. Conversely, fire destroys metal and so a commercial enterprise would be wise to avoid this combination.

Metal generates water, thus a metal-element building in a water-element location will result in an outpouring of finance to the surroundings. Such a location would therefore be unsuitable for a bank or similar business but may be acceptable to an organisation such as a media company or possibly some sort of religious centre that benefits from its product naturally finding an effective channel to the outside world. Finally, in an earth-element location, a metal building would be the focus of success, because earth generates metal. This would be ideal for any business, particularly if the building incorporated some circular features or domes.

Fire

The fire location – with mountain peaks or their urban equivalent, steep roofs and buildings with sharp corners – seems to imply a continual restlessness. Although a building and location from this same element can be steady, the need for excitement (*as described earlier, The Five Elements – Fire*) means that it will only be productive for a limited time. For a business, therefore, it may be a good place to start but there will always be the need to contemplate moving.

An especially good combination is that of a fire-element building in a wood-element location.

This is because wood feeds fire and therefore the local surroundings help sustain the business in the fire-element building. The same will apply to a home – and prosperity can be expected from this combination. From the earlier sequence (*see* figure 4) we can see that fire destroys metal and so a fire-element building in a metal-element location will be dominant and this combination should lead to success, whether financial or personal. Thus if there is the potential to move your business to a building with steep roofs and other angular features at a location with a predominance of domes, arches etc, then it could be your key to success! The exact opposite is true of the fire building in a water location, because water puts out fire and this would not be a very auspicious place to start a business. The water may be represented by natural water as in streams and lakes or manmade watersides as found at the docks or by canals. Buildings at a water-element location would have a strange shape with no set pattern and rounded edges.

Finally, fire generates earth (as represented by the ashes left after the fire) and so this combination is a good one. A fire-element building will be readily seen in an earth element location and will be something of a focal point and will be beneficial for the area. A good example of such a building in this area would be a hospital or community centre. A business would do well enough, but perhaps more importantly, it would be a beneficiary to the community.

Water

Buildings that fall under this element are, as stated above, irregular in shape, often with a lot of glass in their construction. They tend not to be symmetrical as with many other buildings and often show flowing lines. This means that the water-element type of building is not seen very often. Although the water-element location can be represented by rolling hills, it usually refers directly to a body of water nearby. This combination would be quite good as it confers constancy while allowing changes to occur – thus adapting to changing circumstances. A water-element building in a wood-element location would be subject to the relationship between the elements, that is, the water would feed the wood. Such a building would therefore be better put to a community use. A similarly beneficial result, although at more of a personal level, would be a water-element building in a metal-element location. This is because metal generates water, resulting in a continued inpouring of good things with the resultant spin-off being prosperity and wellbeing.

A less propitious combination would be that of a water-element building in a fire-element location. In physical terms the water type of building would not mix well with buildings of the fire type and in Feng Shui terms the water would destroy the fire. This would almost certainly result in friction as the occupants of the water-element building became dominant in the area, thus antagonising neighbours. This would happen however justified or unjustified the neighbours were. Because earth destroys water, an earth-element type of location would not be a good choice for a water-element building. The water would be soiled by the earth leading possibly to tarnished reputations and generally negative influences.

Earth

Although many buildings are made of brick and/or concrete and therefore have some link with the earth element, it is more the shape of the building than the materials of which it is built that matter. Thus a low perspective building with a flat roof would be typical. In an earth-element location, such a building provides a rock-steady base but one from which there are unlikely to be many earth-shattering developments. That, however, might suit a great many people! Wood 'destroys' the earth (taking nourishment from it) and so although this arrangement (earth-element building in wood-element location) may at first sight seem acceptable, in fact it will lead to a depletion of resources, both personal and financial and should not be endured for too long.

Because earth generates metal, an earth-element building in a metal-element location should again be the sort of building that houses an activity of benefit to the community. There would be a continual outpouring of resources that would not suit a business or anyone who needed to save their meagre funds. The opposite is true of a earth-element building in a fire-element location; fire generates earth and therefore this creates a positive effect for those living or working in this set-up. Not only that, the combination is ongoing and productive and so would lend itself to almost any type of use. In a water element location, the earth-element building benefits from the dominance of earth over water but the water location will suffer. Thus success may come at the expense of those nearby or the environment.

The use of the five elements in moderating elemental conflicts

When a building, be it house, office or factory, of a particular element type is located in an area under another element, and one which will confer a negative influence, it is possible to offset the bad influence by use of one of the remaining elements. This is based upon the cycle of moderation mentioned earlier (*see* Implications of the Five Elements) and an example would be:

Wood moderates between water and fire

So if a fire element building were located in a water-element area – not a good combination as explained above – it would be possible to ameliorate the situation by introducing wood which supports fire because wood feeds fire. An alternative would be to introduce earth which destroys water. In each such case, there would be a moderating factor which either generates the element being destroyed or destroys the element that is threatening.

The moderating factor can be represented in many different ways from something simple such as an aquarium to introduce water to something more complex, perhaps introducing wood into the fire/water situation mentioned above such that the wood feeds the fire. In a practical way this could involve the use of the colour associated with wood (green or blue, but not dark blue), introduction of wood inside the building by means of screens, decorations or even just more wooden items such as furniture or surrounds. Outside the building, trees could be planted in strategic places, but it would be necessary to ensure this was done correctly (that is, do not plant to the south or outside windows) as mentioned elsewhere in this book.

We shall now consider briefly the moderating influence of the remaining elements, as specified earlier in the text, and provide general guidance on how this can be achieved. The relationships can be appreciated simply and graphically by consulting figure 4.

Fire moderates between wood and earth

Wood hinders earth but fire helps earth, so the introduction of a fire-related element will support earth. Fire can be introduced in many ways. Firstly, if considering the interior layout of a house, a nice open fire could be all that is required. Fire is also represented by the colour red and so the use of this colour in the decoration or in carpets, curtains or borders would all help in this situation. Externally there is less that can be done. Because fire is represented by spires, towers and steep roofs, it is unlikely that a building will be modified to the extent of changing the roof. If an extension is being added to the house, or a garage being constructed, then a pitched roof would be the obvious choice in this respect.

Earth moderates between fire and metal

Of course fire melts metal, so because earth supports metal (and fire helps earth) this is the ideal moderating influence. The same applies where water extinguishes fire – because earth absorbs water. This situation may be represented by a metal-element building (rounded form) in a fire-element location (sharp hills or mountains; or steep roofed buildings and tower blocks etc.). Introducing earth can be achieved by introducing the material itself by means of a small construction – whether a wall, decorative tiles, or the use of an appropriate colour which in this case may be a brown, yellow or orange.

Metal moderates between earth and water

Looking once more at the sequences of generation and destruction, we see that earth destroys water. However, metal generates water (*see* figure 4) so this is the moderating influence. Metal can also moderate between earth and wood, when earth is threatened by wood because metal cuts wood. Inside a building, metal can be introduced quite simply and in a number of ways. The material itself can be used, perhaps by means of some wrought iron or through the strategic placing of a set of candlesticks. (If fire is also required, then this is the standard way of introducing both elements – candlesticks and candles.) Internal decoration can be altered to use the colours of metal which are white, grey, silver and similar. Externally it may be feasible to erect railings around a garden, a metal archway over which plants can trail, or if the budget can extend to it (or if you are a sculptor) to place a metal sculpture in the garden. This type of solution would be particularly appropriate to a water-element building in an earth-element location.

Water moderates between metal and wood

As you will no doubt appreciate by now, metal destroys wood – it cuts it and therefore water has to be introduced because water supports wood. Water can also be used as a moderating influence when fire and metal are in conflict. Fire melts metal, but of course water extinguishes fire. It is relatively straightforward to introduce water to a location. Internally this can be achieved by installing an aquarium, probably a better solution than adopting the colours of water which are dark blues, black, etc. It is unlikely that you will wish to paint your walls or ceiling in such dark colours, but this could be managed by the introduction of dark panels on doors, using a dark border on the walls or by placing a dark blue rug in the appropriate place. As already mentioned, a dark rug can be taken to represent a body of water and is a simple way of bringing water into the situation.

If the building is a commercial premises then it may be possible to introduce water by means of a fountain or even a small pond with fish, probably in the entrance area. Outside, whether considering domestic or commercial premises, it is much easier to construct a fountain, pond, or to utilise a stream.

These are merely some basic suggestions to indicate the sort of approach to be adopted when some moderating influence is required. As already stated, quite often a combination of influences is required but this can be achieved quite easily, as shown by the example of candles and candlestick. Another common solution is to have an aquarium and red fish when fire and water elements are necessary. In many cases, the item can be something simple and ordinary. Here are some other combinations that may prove useful, but this is only an indication, the list is certainly not exhaustive:

Combination of elements required	Possible solution
fire and metal	candles and candlestick stoves of various descriptions
wood and metal	metal chairs with wooden arms, etc. wrought iron trellis painted green or blue (the colour for wood) a metal tool with a wooden handle

Combination of elements required	Possible solution
wood and earth	a display of dried flowers in a stoneware vase
	a wooden framed painting with autumnal colours
water and fire	candles floating on water
wood and fire	an open log fire with log stack
	a wooden screen with red details/picture
earth and metal	small indoor garden in a metal trough
	ornaments of metal coloured in earth colours (gold, brass, or another metal painted appropriately)
water and wood	wooden ornament painted in the colours of water
	aquatic plant

A Broader Perspective

Before turning to the workings and applications of Feng Shui it is interesting to note another aspect of the subject that is an extension of the pictorial representation of yin and yang. This is the concept of trigrams and their use in the presentation of the seasons and compass directions. It should be stated here that practitioners of Feng Shui quite often work in ways that are slightly different from each other. This is quite normal and to be expected, but some aspects of the subject may therefore differ between experts. Some incorporate a significant amount of astrology into their application of Feng Shui, others do not while others place considerable emphasis on the use of trigrams, hexagrams and the link between Feng Shui and the *I Ching* (the *Book Of Changes*). In this book, a straightforward and relatively simple, descriptive account is presented to enable the reader to grasp the basics. Anyone who then wishes to delve more deeply into the subject can do so by means of the many sources now available.

Seasons and trigrams

From yin and yang to trigrams and I Ching

Developing from the use of yin and yang lines of the oracle, it became necessary to provide a greater flexibility and differentiation other than just yes and no. By combining the two lines to give all available permutations, four pairs of lines were produced (*as in* figure 5) and later a third line was added to give the eight symbols, called trigrams (*see* figure 6). These trigrams symbolised all that happens in earth and heaven and they were all thought to be constantly changing into each other thus representing the continual and transitional state of affairs in the real world. Each trigram has a particular name relating to natural processes in the world as listed opposite (*also refer to* figure 6):

Figure 5

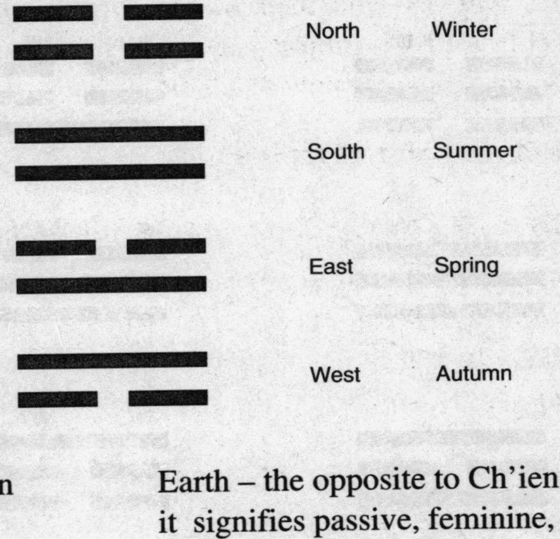

K'un	Earth – the opposite to Ch'ien; it signifies passive, feminine, kindness and devotion
Ch'ien	Heaven – creatively inspired with strength and vitality but also power, domination and coldness
Li	Fire – represents beauty and enlightenment and also clinging

Figure 6 – the eight trigrams used in I Ching and Feng Shui

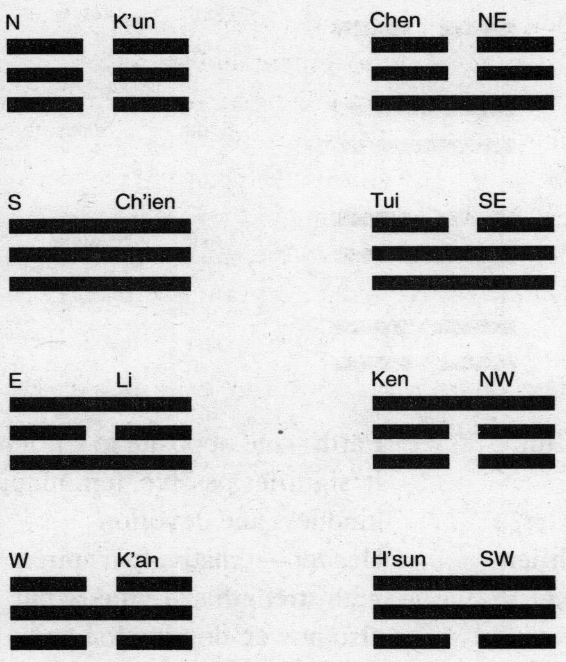

K'an	Water – signifies deep thought and concentration and also danger
Chen	Thunder – this relates to movement and represents growth, being impulsive
Tui	Marsh – represents growth, joy, success and sensual pleasure
Ken	Mountain – represents calm, caution and thoroughness
H'sun (or sun)	Wind – signifies growth and animal life, flexibility

The eight trigrams are further classified into major and minor trigrams based upon the combination of their lines, yang being strong and yin being yielding. The categories are as follows:

major yang trigrams – Ch'ien and Tui
major yin trigrams – K'un and Ken
minor yang trigrams – K'an and H'sun
minor yin trigrams – Chen and Li

As will be appreciated, each trigram has a

particular characteristic, thus heaven is creative and is yang. Different meanings are also attributed to the trigrams with respect to the natural phenomena in the world. Different trigrams are also associated with the different roles of family members. The table opposite lists the trigrams and their main associations.

The eight primary trigrams in combination generate the sixty-four (eight times eight) hexagrams of the I Ching. Each hexagram (*see* figure 7) is thus composed of an upper and lower trigram, but in addition the internal trigrams (i.e. lines 2, 3 and 4, 4 and 5 from the top) which are called the nuclear trigrams. The analysis of these trigrams is the key to the study of I Ching.

Figure 7 – a typical hexagram

The main associations of the eight trigrams

Name	*Ch'ien*	*K'un*	*Chen*	*K'an*	*Ken*	*H'sun*	*Li*	*Tui*
Means	heaven	earth	thunder	water	mountain	wind	fire	marsh
Traits	creative/ strong	receptive/ yielding	arousing/ moving	danger	resting	gentle	separate	joyful
Animal	horse	cow	dragon	pig	dog	cat	bird	sheep
Season	early winter	early autumn	spring	winter	early spring	early summer	summer	autumn
Polarity	yang	yin	yang	yang	yang	yin	yin	yin
Element	metal	soil	grass	wood	stone	air	fire	flesh
Direction	NW	SW	E	N	NE	SE	S	W
Family	father	mother	first son	middle son	third son	first daughter	second daughter	third daughter
Colour	purple	black	orange	red	green	white	yellow	blue
Part of Body	head	solar plexus	foot	ear	hand	thighs	eye	mouth

The numbers which refer to the 64 hexagrams in I Ching

	Chi'en	**K'un**	**Chen**	**K'an**	**Ken**	**H'sun**	**Tui**	**Li**
Chi'en	1	11	34	5	26	9	43	14
K'un	12	2	16	8	23	20	45	35
Chen	25	24	51	3	27	42	17	21
K'an	6	7	40	29	4	59	47	64
Ken	33	15	62	39	52	53	31	56
H'sun	44	46	32	48	18	57	28	50
Tui	10	19	54	60	41	61	58	38
Li	13	36	55	63	22	37	49	30

The sixty four hexagrams are thus made up of the combinations of the two primary trigrams (*see* table opposite).

Each number can be looked up in a book on the I Ching to provide a full analysis. Each hexagram is interpreted to assist the individual who is consulting the I Ching to gain guidance. Below is one such example for hexagram 7, Shih, The Army.

Hexagram 7

Component trigrams: Primary: K'un (upper); K'an (lower); Nuclear: K'un (above); Chen (below)
Keywords: Earth, water, firmness, authority, group action, danger, dissension, devotion
Commentary: There is a lack of harmony in your present situation, with contending forces causing confusion and unrest. But if you show firmness of purpose and keep your eye steadily on a goal which is worthy of attainment then you will succeed. Your exemplary action will transform aimless confusion into co-ordination

and a worthwhile sense of direction. You will be an inspiration and a guide to others and will command their respect and admiration. With their help and support you will attain a position of distinction.

Judgement: With firmness and correctness and a leader of age and experience, there will be good fortune and no error.

A group of soldiers requires a steady and competent leader to unite them and keep them in good order. The leader must eliminate grievance and injustice and ensure instead that justice and peaceful concord prevail in the group. In and through this leadership endeavour he will command the respect, loyalty and love of his soldiers. The implication is that you should recruit the enthusiastic help and support of those around you to work together for a worthwhile common goal.

Interpretation: The only solid line in the hexagram is found in the middle line of the lower primary trigram. This gives rise to the image of a general who is the commander of the broken yin lines. This hexagram is about proper discipline, good order and legitimate and worthy power. It shows that an effective army requires effective soldiers and leadership. The good army remains in a state of prepared readiness until action is necessary, when it responds with spirit and alacrity. In a situation of conflict there is always the possibility of civil insurrection, but if the people are treated properly they will contribute to the size of the army.

Image: Water in the midst of the earth. The wise ruler nourishes and educates the people and collects from among them the multitude of his army. A ruler must instil a respect and desire for justice, good authority and harmony in his people by his own merits and example, commanding love and respect for his kindness, strength and unstinting support.

Line readings: *Line 1*: The army goes forth according to the proper rules. If these are not good there will be misfortune. (Success depends on the right motivation and the best preparation. Take a good and honest look at yourself.)

Line 2: The leader is in the middle of the army. There will be good fortune and no error. The king has thrice conveyed to him the orders of his favour. (You are awarded a distinction which is merited by the respect those around you have for your good judgement and successful work. They share in the credit and honour, as you all work together in a situation of mutual respect.)

Line 3: The army may have many inefficient leaders. There will be misfortune. (Be honest and vigilant about your faults and weaknesses otherwise your endeavour will end in failure. Maintain a perceptive and judicious sense of authority and control over yourself and others.)

Line 4: The army is in retreat. There is no error. (Now is the time to make a tactical retreat from a situation. You are not capitulating but surviving to fight again another day. Wait until a more advantageous time arrives. Be patient.)

Line 5: There are birds in the fields which it

will be advantageous to seize and destroy. There will be no error. If the oldest son leads the army, and younger men idly occupy offices assigned to them, then however firm and correct he may be, there will be misfortune. (Success requires maturity. You must compensate for the immaturity of yourself and your advisers by seeking out those who can give wise and mature guidance. Guard against the mistake of confusing age with wisdom.)

Line 6: The king gives his rewards, appointing some to be rulers of states, and others to undertake the headship of clans; but small men should not be employed. (You have achieved success but don't bask unthinkingly in your moment of glory. You should take time to survey and assess the nature and merits of your attainment with a scrupulous honesty. Ask yourself if you are where you deserve to be and where you want to be, and whether you are better, morally and practically, than the person you have replaced. Be true to yourself.

The I Ching is consulted by phrasing a question, which must be serious and genuine in nature, and which requires a yes or no response. The significance of the hexagrams rests with their symbolism and interpretation. Each represents a transitional state in life and all the hexagrams together represent a sequence of situations in life. Within the hexagram itself, it is the modification and movement of the yin and yang lines that change one hexagram into another.

Each hexagram has a Chinese name and a translation and its analysis falls into three categories: the Judgement, the Image, Line Readings and the Interpretation. The Judgement presents the overall theme and meaning of the hexagram with its good or bad fortune. The Image looks at the symbolic nature of the hexagram and the analysis of each individual line. (In these hexagrams, only the lines that are termed 'moving lines' are important – any text on I Ching will provide a full explanation.) The Interpretation gives an explanatory account of the Judgement and the structure of the hexagram. Each hexagram is preceded by a Commentary which summarises the overall meaning.

Origin of the trigrams

The trigrams are believed to have been created by the first Chinese emperor, Fu His, around 3000 BC. He was a teacher and a scholar and it is thought to have been his life's work. The work of Fu His was expanded and rearranged some 2000 years later by the founder of the Chou dynasty, King Wen. At about this time, King Wen and his son the Duke of Chou expanded the trigrams into the six line hexagrams. A particular name was given to each hexagram and information was provided for each one, giving advice and a commentary which was known as the *T'uan* or the *Judgement*. There is also text (called the *Hsiang Chuan* or *Image*) based upon the lines of each hexagram and probably much of the text came from a number of authors.

In the early fifth century, further commentaries were added and this has continued over history, notably by the philosopher Chu His during the Sung dynasty (960–1279). The I Ching first reached the west in the early 1700s but a German missionary, Richard Wilhelm, discovered it in China in the late nineteenth century and after translation into German, it formed the basis for subsequent English translations.

Trigrams in Feng Shui

Feng Shui uses the basic linear representations of yin and yang, and the trigrams, although the names and interpretations may differ a little. Commencing with the broken and solid lines of yin and yang two further designs were generated to represent east and west. As we have already seen, yin stands for north and yang for south. Because yang is sun, light, heaven and all things that tend upwards, yang and south are portrayed as being to the top, thus where we in the west would expect north to be uppermost, in the case of Feng Shui it is the opposite. By using combinations of the two basic symbols, the four new designs can now be allocated to the compass points and the seasons, as shown. Figure 5 shows their configuration, in each case the design is a different combination of the lines for yin and yang. By developing this system one stage further, adding a third line as described above, another four designs are created which represent the remaining compass points, north east, south west and so on (*as shown in* figure 6). There are now eight symbols, the trigrams, each of which is made up of the characteristic three parallel lines or broken lines, and again the third line added is the line either for yin or yang. Each of the three-lined symbols or trigrams has some significance. In Feng Shui, the top line is the yin or yang, the earth and sky; the central line is the four seasons and points of the compass; the lowest line then represents man.

Each of the trigrams is given a name which is very similar to that described above for the I Ching, and thus each one then has a name, direction and also a trait or representation.

Direction	Name	Season	Representation
North	K'un (Responsive)	Winter	creation
North west	Ken (Calm)		mountain
West	K'an (Hazardous)	Autumn	moon
South west	H'sun (Wind)		gentle
South	Ch'ien (Inventive)	Summer	heaven
South east	Tui (Lake)		joy
East	Li (Clinging)	Spring	sun
North east	Chen (Stimulating)		thunder

The Former Heaven Sequence or Pah Kwa

When these eight trigrams are placed around the compass they create a symbol called the *Pah Kwa* or the *Former Heaven Sequence*, and this octagonal arrangement is considered very lucky by the Chinese (*see* figure 8). This pattern is

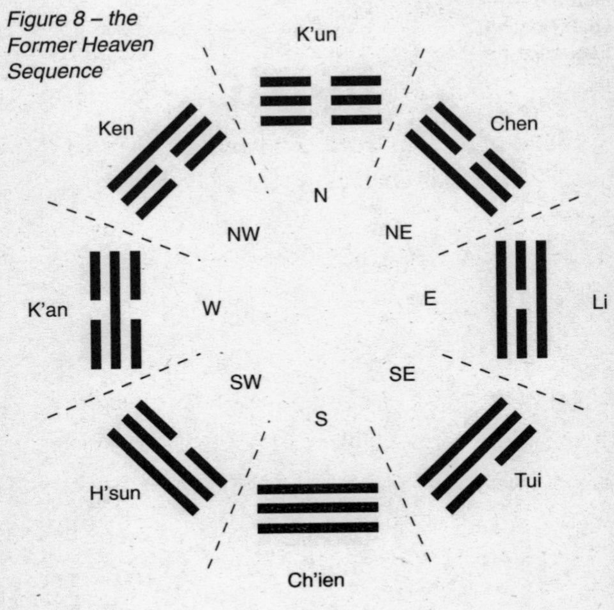

Figure 8 – the Former Heaven Sequence

found on mirrors to combat sha chi and it is also used in 'good luck' charms or talismans. A slightly different form, the Later Heaven Sequence (*see* figure 9) is used on mariners' compasses in China. Each trigram has a certain position but the position itself changes between the

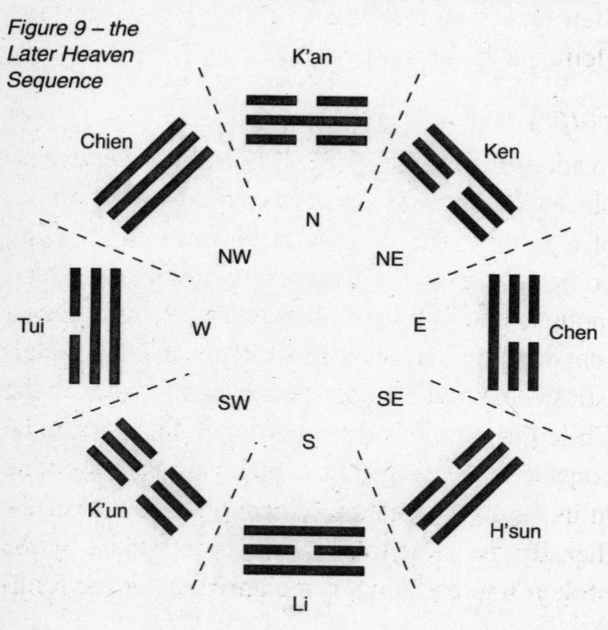

Figure 9 – the Later Heaven Sequence

two sequences. The name of each trigram is constant and what it represents (*see* table on page 90) also remains the same.

Also at the cardinal points of the compass in Feng Shui are usually depicted one of the four elements, water, fire, metal and wood. Earth is then placed in the centre. This gives us the five elements as discussed previously.

Family associations

In addition to the properties shown in the above table, each trigram is also associated with a member of a family. The core of any family, its starting point, is that of the man and woman, father and mother. You will recall that unbroken lines represent yang and among the attributes and characteristics is the male gender. Accordingly, because the Ch'ien trigram has three unbroken lines, it can be considered to be the one which is most masculine in its nature and naturally occupies the role of father. By the same token, yin is represented by the broken line and among the attributes is the feminine gender. In this case, it is K'un which has three broken lines and is therefore the most feminine and thus represents mother.

This analysis can be extended to incorporate the larger family. The trigram K'an has a central unbroken line bounded by broken lines top and bottom, implying a male with thin females. This is taken to represent the middle son and the converse applies to Li where the centre line is broken, hence this is the middle daughter. The trigrams with a broken and unbroken line at the base are the eldest daughter and eldest son respectively (the H'sun and Chen trigrams). The table below summarises this sequence and also shows the element attributed to each.

Trigram	Family Member	Element
Ch'ien	Father	metal
K'un	Mother	earth
Chen	Eldest son	wood
H'sun	Eldest daughter	wood
K'an	Middle son	water
Li	Middle daughter	fire
Ken	Youngest son	earth
Tui	Youngest daughter	metal

The Magic Square

If the octagonal shape of the Pah Kwa mentioned above is drawn out until the lines impinge upon a square, the result is what is called the magic square or Lo Shu. This has its basis

Figure 10 – generating the Magic Square, Lo Shu, from the Pah Kwa, and the positions of the numbers

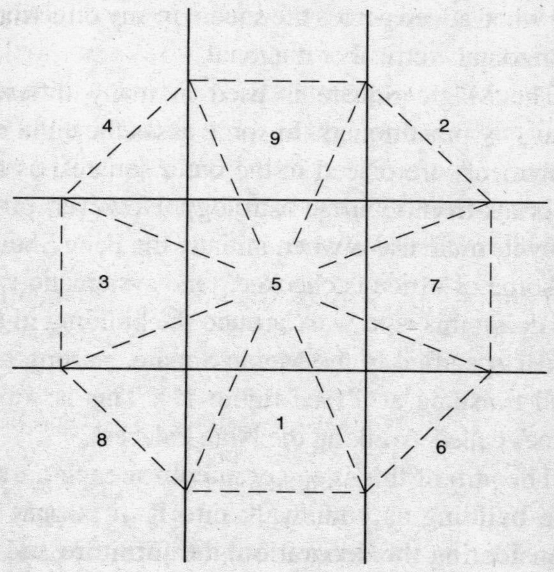

also in numerology, the study of numbers and their significance, where it is found that all numbers, when their individual digits are summed, can eventually be reduced to a number between 1 and 9. The use of this square in China goes back a very long way and cannot truly be traced. As can be seen from figure 10, the numbers form a total of 15 when added across the square in any direction – horizontal, vertical or diagonal.

The Magic Square is used in many different ways by practitioners. In some cases the eight endowments are placed in the outer squares, as are animals from Chinese astrology. However, probably its main use is when initially the Feng Shui of a home or office is checked. One systematic way of doing this is to walk around the building in the order specified in the Magic Square, starting at 1 and finishing at 9 (*see* figure 11). This is sometimes called 'Walking the Nine Palaces'.

The aim of this is to get a feel for each part of the building as your walk into it. It is only by considering the decoration, the furniture and its

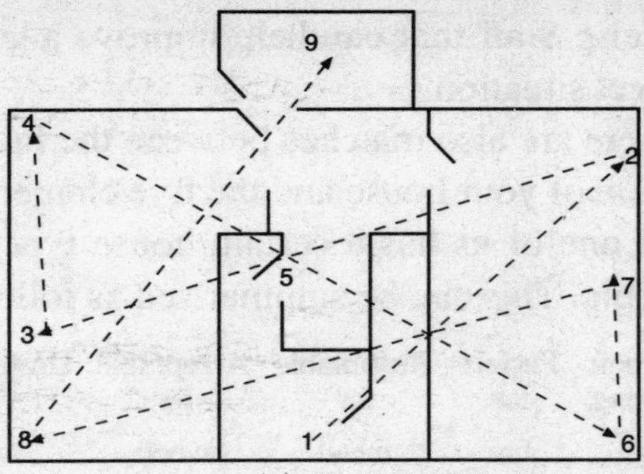

Figure 11 – applying the magic square to checking out the Feng Shui of a building

position, the general atmosphere of the area and what it is used for and how it is used that any improvements can be made. For example, there may be improvements in decor, type and placement of furniture and other items that could be made to improve the overall Feng Shui of the area and building. Upon finishing the process at the front door, the ideal situation would be to face south or south-east. but this will usually not be possible. However, this is not critical and there are many aspects of Feng Shui that can help improve a less than perfect situation.

There are also matches between the facing direction of your house and the five elements, and each one of us has a certain house type that is suitable. This can be summarised as follows:

Direction of Facing	Perfect for	Reasonable for	Acceptable for	Unsuitable for for
North	fire	metal	wood	water
South	water	wood	metal	fire
East	wood	fire	water	metal
West	metal	water	fire	wood

Earth types are not included because the direction has less impact upon them and they can live almost anywhere. In terms of the house types, that is, the type to match the occupants, the general guide is:

wood – practical, unusual
earth – family, congenial
metal – organised, modern
water – conservative, quiet
fire – warm, comfortable

(*See also* the sections on each of the five elements.)

The Workings of Feng Shui

Introduction

Although the essential workings of Feng Shui are relatively straightforward and can be applied logically, different practitioners and groups of practitioners develop particular strengths and ways of working which in time become rules to follow. Because this has led to available accounts of the subject appearing quite different in many respects, we shall in this book attempt to bring together the main ways of working with Feng Shui. Thus, although there may well be additional aspects of a technique that are not covered here or are referred to only in passing, the interested reader will be able to grasp the fundamentals and undertake their own research in depth, using the growing library of books and information sources now available.

By studying the various attributes of a living space, its Feng Shui can be determined, good Feng Shui can be enhanced further and bad Feng Shui can be corrected. This can apply equally to the home, garden or business premises. There are a number of techniques and actions that can be adopted and implemented to improve the Feng Shui, including the use of light, colour and linear features. Some Feng Shui consultants call these the eight remedies; here they are referred to under the general heading of 'restorative action'. In all cases, the aim is to balance the chi, by altering, increasing or reducing it in some way.

To redress poor Feng Shui situations, attention can be paid to chi and sha chi and the countermeasures that can be employed or the focus can be the five elements, and the need to achieve a balance. The five elements have been considered above, with their inter-relationships and moderating combinations. Some indications have been given of actions that can be taken to correct imbalances and conflicts and from this the general principles and practices can be determined.

When it comes to chi within the building, the primary objective is to encourage the good chi and keep out the sha chi. The chi is meant to flow around the building in a gentle fashion, unhindered by obstacles and general untidiness. The beneficial currents of chi should enter by the main door and circulate throughout the house, leaving by a window or the back entrance. On its way around the house, it should really pass through every room. When checking a house to ensure it has the optimum arrangement for the flow of chi, it should be possible to visualise a flow entering by the main door and then branching and flowing around each floor and up the stairs to the next floor. As it flows it divides to enter the various rooms with one flow continuing around the house. In this way the chi can go into each room through the door and exit either by a second door or by a window, but not by the same entrance through which it entered the room. Doors should open inwards to encourage the flow (other stipulations concerning doors are considered in the appropriate section).

Specific topics and measures are dealt with but a few general principles can be mentioned here. It is important that the chi has the opportunity to flow around the room before leaving – if it leaves too quickly there is little opportunity for the chi to stimulate the room space. The rapid loss of chi can happen in many circumstances:

- where there are windows at opposite ends of the room
- when the stairs descend directly towards the front door
- when a house is 'divided' by a central corridor, with the back door visible from the front

Each of these cases, and the necessary remedial action that can be taken, is described in full elsewhere.

In addition to losing chi, there are many spaces in buildings that are, to all intents and purposes, dead areas. This is when the flow of chi is stopped, either in the corners of rooms or in rooms without windows or a suitable exit point for the chi. The corners of rooms can easily be dealt with, as specifically indicated in other sections, by placing plants, ornaments and similar items in the space. Rooms that are effectively closed systems are best relegated to use as store rooms and cupboards but it does help if the door opens outwards in these cases, the contrary to what is normally required. Quite often garages (those attached to houses) are dead spaces. It will help to have a back door as well as the main entrance. However, if a bedroom is built above a garage which is a dead space there is the possibility that the bedroom will suffer from the dead chi. Other 'closed' buildings, such as halls of certain types or cinemas where there are not meant to be any windows, may also suffer in this respect but outward-opening doors will help.

Restorative action

When a consultant first assesses a building they may well use a Feng Shui compass, which consists of a board with a magnetic needle sited at the centre. Around this is a number of concentric circles, commonly over twenty. Contained within each ring is information that is of relevance to the Feng Shui diagnosis. The rings are set in a square-base board, thus creating a parallel with yin and yang, earth and heaven, square and circle, because the inner circular part is called the Heaven Plate and the outer square component is the Earth Plate. The compass is used by aligning it with the orientation of the building in question and information is taken from the circular parts. Further information is gleaned after matching the building with the individual's horoscope. This results in a pair of readings that usually indicate that some corrective measures are necessary. The eight categories may be used independently or together in varying amounts.

Methods of restorative action

Light and mirrors
Colour
Linear features
Acoustic measures
Flora and fauna
Static elements
Motion
Equipment

Light and mirrors

Perhaps the commonest and most used method of restorative action in Feng Shui, is the employment of light, mirrors and other surfaces that may reflect light in a similar way. In general, lights should be quite bright but should not be too glaring. In China, light is often used in the garden and around the outside of the house. Mirrors can be used just about anywhere and enable dark rooms to be illuminated well, including corners that without a direct source of light would remain dark. Mirrors enable bad chi to be directed back out of a building or by locating them in particular positions, good chi can be brought in by enlightening a particular aspect of the room, or by reflecting a pleasant view from outside, perhaps a snapshot of the garden or a body of water. Chi can be directed into corners and, by the prudent use of light and mirrors, a room can be improved immeasurably. Mirrors also encourage the flow of chi around the room and are therefore positioned in the dead spaces or where the flow of chi would otherwise stop.

It should also be remembered that too many mirrors can be a bad thing in certain rooms. For example, in the bedroom where there should be a restful atmosphere, too many mirrors can energise the chi too much, causing sleepless nights. Also, a lounge need not have many mirrors.

Colour

Many people tend to decorate their house with relatively quiet colours and perhaps only the younger generations opt for strong, loud colour schemes. However, colours can be used to help the flow of chi and an area of bright colour in an otherwise dull room can help enormously. The Chinese certainly follow this practice and commonly use red and black as these are deemed particularly fortuitous when it comes to financial matters. Aspects of the use of colour in Feng Shui will be considered later in the book.

Linear features

When it becomes necessary to divert the flow of chi, as often happens when it moves too quickly, for example, in long corridors, linear features can be very useful. The feature may be a fan, sword, bamboo tube or one of a number of items that are placed at an angle (across the corridor) to redirect the chi back into rooms.

Acoustic measures

Noise, particularly melodic, harmonious sounds, can break up chi that has become sluggish because they generate sound waves in the air. Many people like wind chimes and without appreciating how they can help, suspend them in their porch or kitchen. Wind chimes, bells, mobiles that create some sort of musical tinkling are all useful in this respect. In addition to moving chi, musical noises are also said to foster wealth by attracting lucky chi into a building.

Flora and fauna

Living things in general can be very useful to move or slow down chi, and this includes plants and also, for example, fish. Plants can be placed in areas where there is no chi, and in locations where the chi needs to be moved around. Furthermore, large plants will slow down chi when it is moving too quickly. Fish in an aquarium can also be useful to slow chi, in addition to providing an interesting and sometimes almost hypnotic focus.

Static elements

This generally applies to features outside where it may become necessary to slow down the flow of chi. This may be the case in a garden and any large object will help compensate. This may be a rock, statue or something similar that slows the chi. If a statue is used it should blend in with the surroundings and with the personality of the individual.

Motion

The movement of an object can help divert or animate chi and the Chinese commonly use items such as flags, ribbons, chimes and mobiles and fountains. Ideally the wind should be the motivating force. Flowing water is helpful in bringing in chi, but it should not flow too rapidly.

Equipment

This includes all types of machine and items of electrical equipment which can vitalise chi, but it is necessary to ensure that it is not overdone. A balance has to be achieved between the electricity which is used in so many modern appliances, from fridges to microwaves to computers, and the chi. The best approach to adopt is to keep such usage to a sensible minimum.

In later sections, the way in which these actions can be applied to Feng Shui will be described. There are numerous examples of such applications throughout the book, particularly when a moderating element is required.

Symbolic animals

In addition to all the other factors involved in Feng Shui there are aspects of astrology and astronomy involved. Four terms derived from Chinese astronomy are used in Feng Shui, being placed at the points of the compass. These four animals, the tortoise (or turtle), bird, dragon and tiger are also associated with directions as applied to a house, and with the seasons. Each animal (often called a celestial animal) has particular

The four celestial animals

associations in terms of character and emotions. These are shown in greater detail in the table shown opposite.

These animal symbols are used to assess the Feng Shui of a house with respect to its position. When a house faces south, into the realm of the red phoenix, then the terms front, back, etc. coincide with the compass directions, i.e. looking out of the house to the south means you are also facing away from the front.

Leaving your house to go into the realm of the red bird is supposed to bring good luck and good fortune. In China it is common practice for people to seek a house that is either south or south-east facing. This is an auspicious set-up as it allows into the house the good fortune of the bird (for south facing) and in addition the wisdom of the dragon (for south-east facing). In front of the house, the ground should gently fall away (*see also* figure 19 and associated text – Door Locations/external doors). If it is too sudden then it is believed that the red bird would fall off and this

The celestial symbolic animals of Feng Shui

Animal	Compass point	Season	Direction of Facing	Colour	Characteristics
tortoise (can also be turtle, or snake; sometimes called warrior)	north	winter	back	black	mysterious, hidden, sleepy, caring
bird (can be any bird, but is often the phoenix)	south	summer	front	red	happy, jovial, lucky, fortunate, outward-going
dragon	east	spring	right	green	wise, kind, safeguarding, polite, good luck
tiger	west	autumn	left	white	sudden, strong, angry, violent, unpredictable

would adversely affect your fortune in the world. With this configuration in mind, the back of the house would be the area of the black tortoise or turtle. This is the area of mystery, but can perhaps be more logically interpreted as the realm of private matters, including marriage and family concerns. Referring again to figure 19, the hills behind the house are necessary to provide protection and keep close at hand all that is of importance at this personal level. To the east ideally there should be hills of the green dragon representing good luck and also hope. To the west is the realm of the white tiger. The land to the west should be flat. Anything else may generate bad luck – hills will mean that the white tiger will be strong with an abundance of the characteristics listed above. This could only lead to problems and difficulties. If the ground to the west rapidly slopes away, then the tiger's effect will be minimal and this can lead to an existence without interest or any excitement. This is the ideal situation but, since this is out of reach for most of us, the Feng Shui of our home interior is important in counteracting any negative aspects outside. This is dealt with later in the book.

The symbolic animals are also used with reference to the walls of the house and the directions in which they face. In a house facing south, the entrance wall is attributed to the bird (compass direction south) but the interior wall facing the entrance is also designated by the bird. However, the outside of that same wall is in the realm of the tortoise because it faces north. By the same token, the other walls can be attributed to the other animals, each being allocated one internal and one external wall dependent upon the direction of facing.

Thus, from this perspective, the best configuration for a house is where the four symbolic animals can be discerned in the outlines of the scenery round about the site. The dragon is regarded as the most important and at the very least it is hoped that a hill to the east can be taken to represent the green dragon. When one of the four animals can be identified in the scenery, then the directions of the other three can obviously be established, even if there are no physical signs of them.

Methods used in Feng Shui

When an individual appraises their home using Feng Shui or when a consultant is called in to a home or office, there are several methods that can be used to sort out the problems. In all cases the result is that the layout of the room will almost certainly be altered and additional items will be installed, as summarised in the preceding section. One method of analysis commonly used is based upon the octagonal structure of the Pah Kwa (*see* Seasons and Trigrams). There are two techniques based upon this basic configuration, one called the *eight point method* and the other, the *eight enrichments* or *endowment method*. The latter consists of laying over the plan of the house in question the octagonal grid (*see* figure 12) and this enables the problem areas to be determined and improvements to be suggested (for convenience this has been shown with the north area to the top). The eight point method involves placing a star made up of eight lines (*see below*) over the plan of the house or individual rooms to see where the lines impinge upon the walls. Both techniques will be described briefly and their application will then be encountered later in this book.

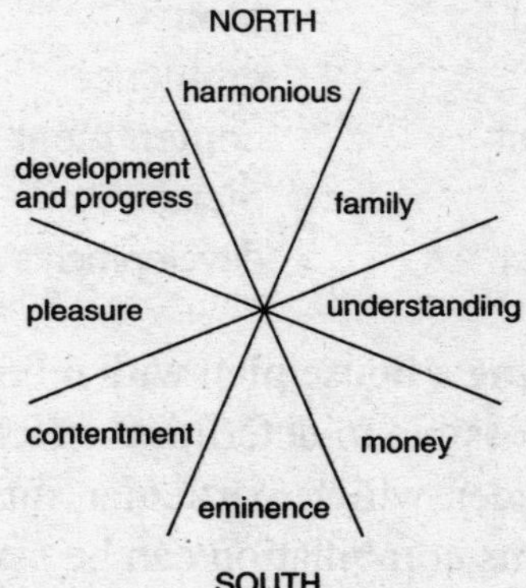

Figure 12 - the areas of the eight enrichments or endowments

The endowment method

This derives its name from the aspect of a person's house. The direction in which it faces enriches the house in a particular way, thus north represents harmonious relationships and east understanding, as listed:

Facing Direction	Endowment
north	harmonious relationships
north east	family
east	understanding
south east	money
south	eminence
south west	contentment
west	pleasure
north west	developments and progress

By studying a house plan with reference to the grid, it is possible to determine which rooms/areas fall under which particular influence and how best this combination can be altered or improved. The grid should always be placed facing south even if the main door to the house does not. The position of the door and its direction of facing is quite important and will be considered in a later section.

The eight point method

This method is used by many practitioners of Feng Shui, and is covered extensively by Simons (*Feng Shui Step by Step*, 1996). In this case the eight-fold grid comprises eight points or areas covering such aspects as, finance,

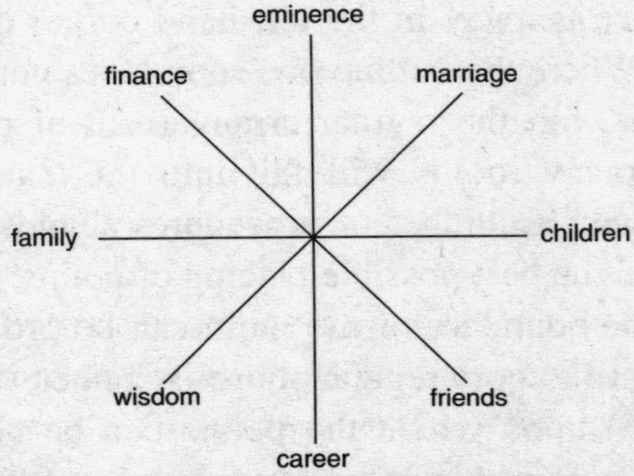

Figure 13 – the grid used in the eight-point method

eminence (or reputation), wisdom (or knowledge), career and so on (*see* figure 13). Once again the grid is placed over the ground plan of the house in question and the wall that contains the main door should also contain the points for knowledge, career and friends. The grid can also be placed over individual rooms and this is often necessary if a house has an unusual ground plan. The placing of the eight points is achieved by standing at the door and imagining that you are looking in, thus eminence is furthest away and finance is away in the left-hand corner (figure 14). Where the outline of a room does not readily fit with the regular arrangement of points, and many rooms will fall into this category, there are a number of procedures suggested to obtain the best possible placing of points:

- The boundary of the room can be projected until a more regular shape is created (figure 15) upon which the points can be placed. However this does not necessarily clarify the placing of points.

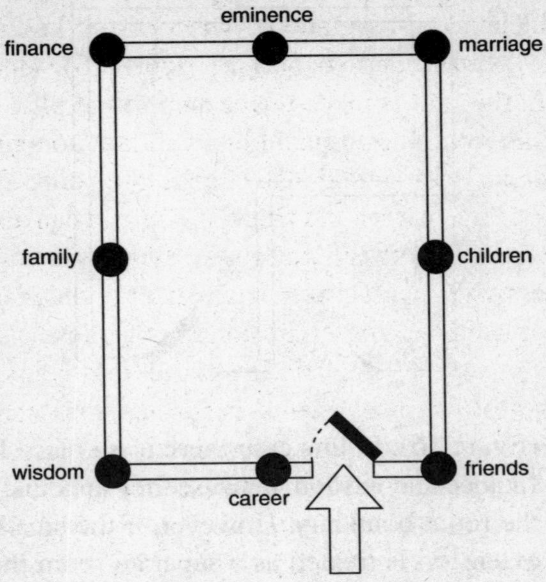

Figure 14 – superimposing the eight points on a room plan

- Where spaces, say in two adjoining rooms, clearly do not accommodate the eight points, it is better to treat them as separate rooms, applying the same principles and standing in each doorway, looking in, to place the points

Figure 15

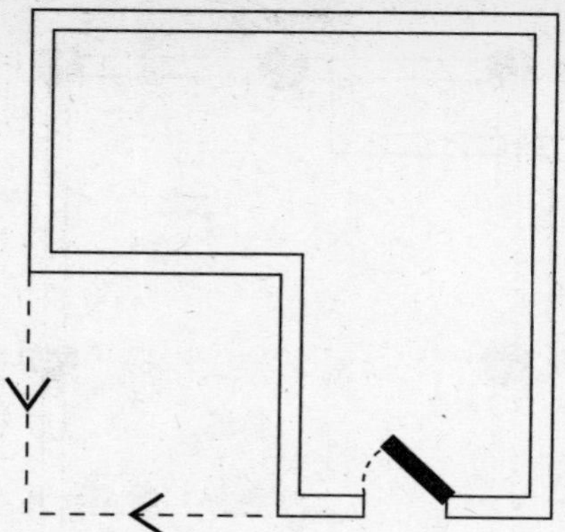

(figure 16). In this case there is no place for finance and wisdom because they are outside the room boundary. However, if the smaller extension is treated as a separate room then all the points can be applied quite easily (figure 17).

- Other rooms may have an irregular shape, which presents you with more than one option for placing the eight points. In this case the points can either be placed to include as much of the space of the room as possible or

Figure 16

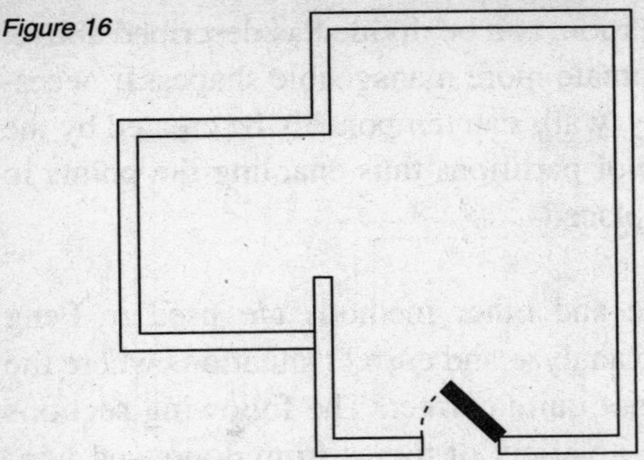

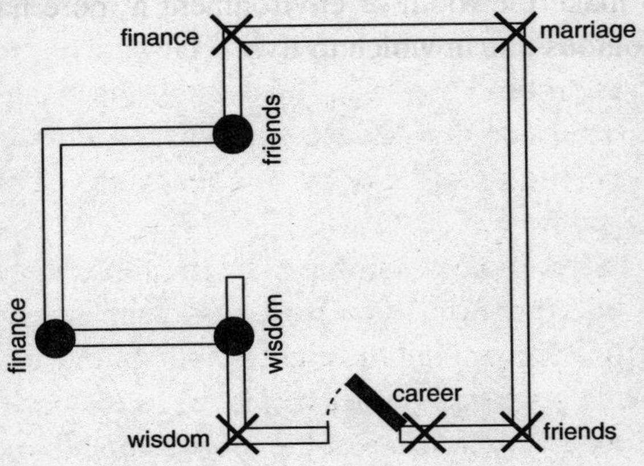

Figure 17 – application of the eight point method to a room extension

the room can be divided as described above, to create more manageable shapes. If necessary, walls can temporarily be created by the use of partitions thus enabling the points to be placed.

These and other methods are used in Feng Shui to analyse and correct situations where the chi is not quite correct. The following sections look at a variety of topics from doors and windows to gardens, pointing out what can be done to make the room or environment a more harmonious one in which to live.

Applying Feng Shui to Building Interiors – At Home

Since the door is the portal, the focus of any building whether a home or an office, that is an appropriate place to start.

Door locations

External doors

Perhaps the most important door is the front door and although it may not be feasible to relocate it to a more beneficial position, it is possible to lessen any deficits. A door that is too large may allow a lot of chi to escape while a door that is too small may need to appear to be larger. To prevent chi escaping, wind chimes, a banner or something similar can be hung by the door to slow down the chi and return it into the building. A doorway can easily be made to appear larger by the careful placing of mirrors. This will also help by reflecting pleasant outside views into the entrance hall (assuming there is a pleasant view to be reflected), porch or room and it should facilitate the escape of bad chi and may enlighten a darker corner in the entrance area, perhaps an area in shadow behind the door. The direction in which the door faces is also important and as already mentioned the most auspicious position is south facing. However, there are many measures that can be taken to improve a less favourable direction of facing.

The door is important in many respects, not least in the view gained on leaving the building and the impression created on entering. It is preferable not to have the door facing objects that are effectively blocking the door, for example, a tree, lamp post, telegraph pole, the corner of another building or a hill. In most cases it is not possible to remedy the situation by removing the obstacle, but this may be feasible with large bushes or small trees which can interfere with the chi. It may, in any case, be advisable to have a tree removed that is very close to your house as the roots could easily disrupt the foundations of the building, particularly in dry weather. The removal of an obstacle to chi will

Figure 18 – balancing obstacles

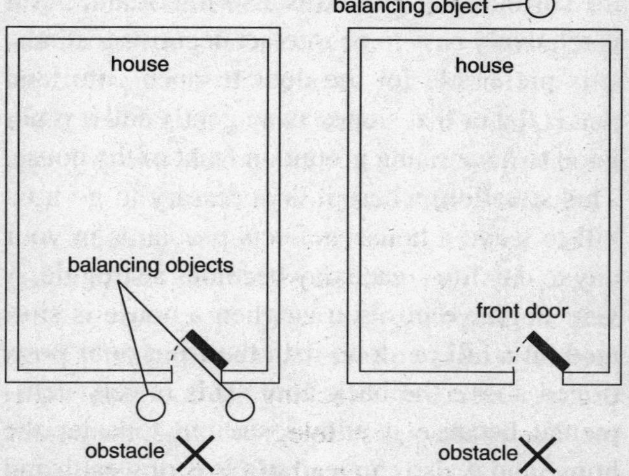

improve your wealth, but if the obstacle cannot be removed, it should be balanced by the careful positioning of other items such as plants, probably in tubs, statues or similar items. An alternative is to place an object behind the house, positioned such that it mirrors the obstacle at the front (*see* figure 18) thus balancing the negative effect.

The position of the main door with respect to the surrounding ground is also important, but it is relatively easy to counteract negative features. It is preferable for the door to open onto land that is flat or that slopes away gently and it is not good to have rising ground in front of the house. This situation, where it is necessary to go up a hill to leave a house, reflects problems in your day to day life – each day becomes a struggle. A very negative position is when a house is situated on a hill or slope with the front door positioned above the back door. This is very detrimental because it allows sha chi to enter the house and it also can lead to a loss of wealth and

Figure 19

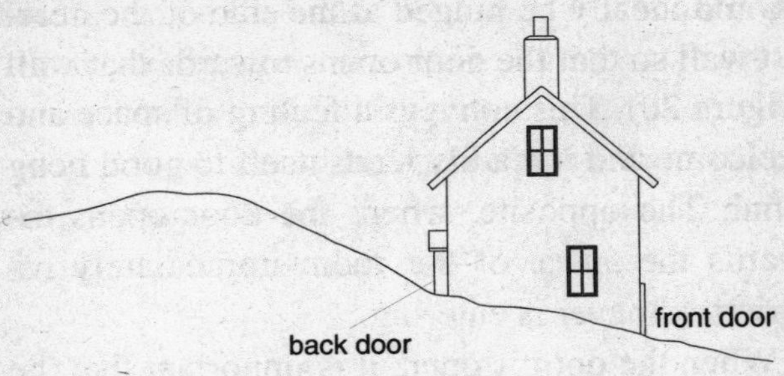

wellbeing. However, there is a very simple and favourable solution that has been adopted in many cases and that is to reverse the doors and use the back door as the main door and vice versa. This creates ideal Feng Shui and this configuration (figure 19) is sometimes called 'sitting on solid ground viewing the sky.' There are also changes that can be made in the approaches to a house that will improve its Feng Shui, for example modifying the paths, and these will be considered in a later section.

When opening the main door into the house, it should ideally be hinged at the side of the nearest wall so that the door opens towards that wall (figure 20). This conveys a feeling of space and welcome and it readily lends itself to good Feng Shui. The opposite, where the door opens towards the space of the room immediately restricts whoever is entering.

When the door is open, it is important that the chi is not allowed to flow straight through the house and out of the back door or a window. This will indeed be the case if, on entering, it is possible to see the back door and this will simply

Figure 20

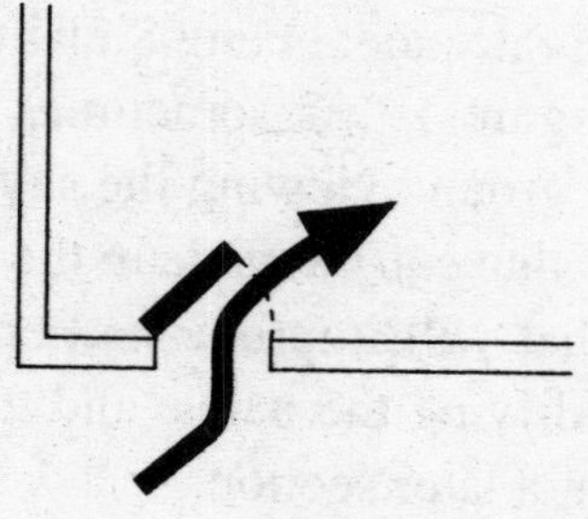

Figure 21

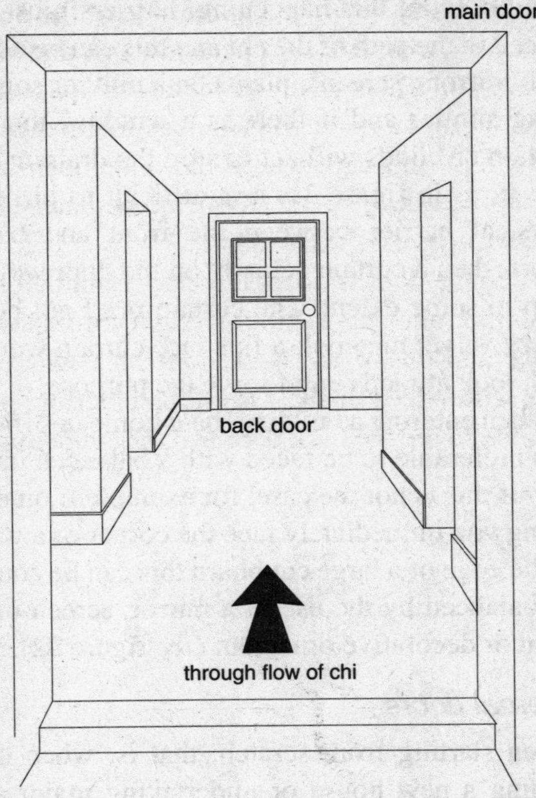
main door
back door
through flow of chi

provide a rapid route for the chi to exit (figure 21). To avoid this happening, barriers must be placed in the path of the chi and this can be done with mirrors, screens, plants on a unit, or something similar and if there is a window, then a curtain or blinds will act to stop the draining of chi. If, as in figure 21, it is difficult to place a physical barrier between the front and back doors, then a curtain actually on the door would help to some extent. The curtain need not be a heavy velvet material, a fine lace curtain would both look attractive and serve the purpose.

When entering a building, be it home or office, it is preferable to be faced with a balanced interior. If this is not the case, for example if on entering you immediately face the corner of a wall or the edge of a large cupboard this can be counter-balanced by the use of a mirror, screen or a plant or decorative ornament (*see* figure 22).

Internal doors

When starting from scratch, that is, when designing a new house or undertaking major al-

Figure 22

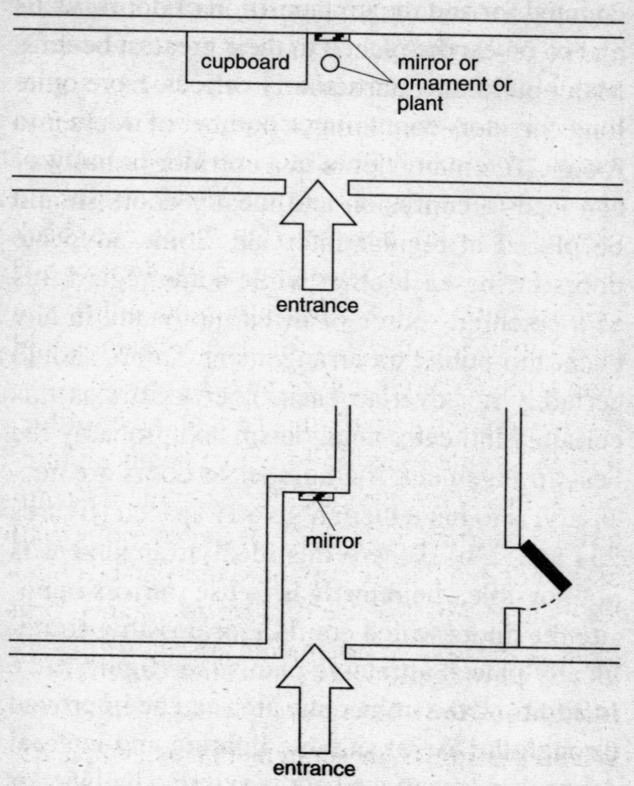
cupboard
mirror or
ornament or
plant
entrance
mirror
entrance

terations, all aspects of Feng Shui can be accounted for and the juxtaposition of doors, walls and so on can be placed to their greatest benefit. Many buildings, particularly offices, have quite long corridors containing a number of doors into rooms. Too many doors in a corridor or hallway can lead to confusion and ideally doors should be placed at regular intervals. Some advocate doors facing each other while some regard this as a potential source of disharmony and in any event too public an arrangement. Doors should certainly not overlap each other a little as this certainly indicates antagonism and probably the best arrangement, if a number of doors are necessary, is to have them regularly spaced (figures 23a and 23b). Where this ideal arrangement is not possible, the remedy is to use mirrors opposite the doors which conflict, or possibly strategically placed attractive plants (*see* figure 23c). In addition, the immediate area can be improved through the use of suitable lighting and internal decor. A room situated at the end of a hallway or

Figure 23

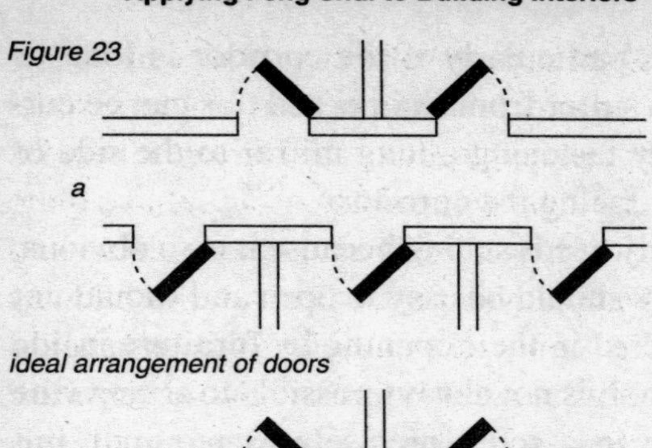

a

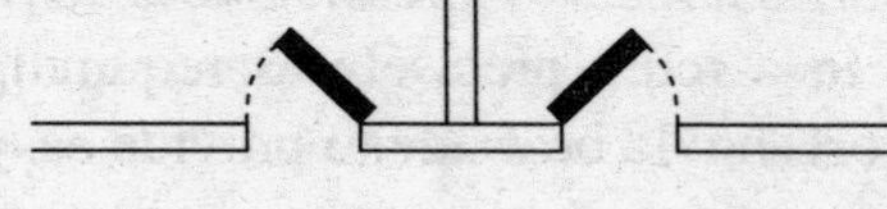

ideal arrangement of doors

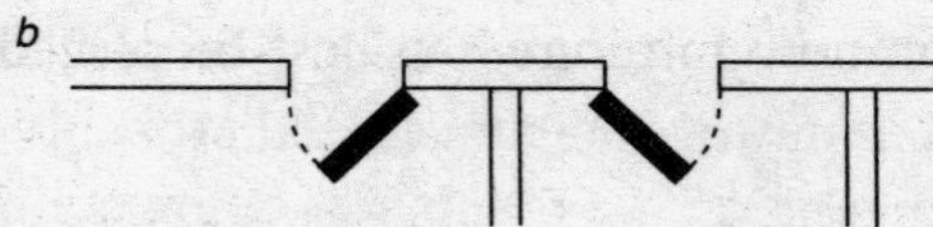

b

good arrangement of doors

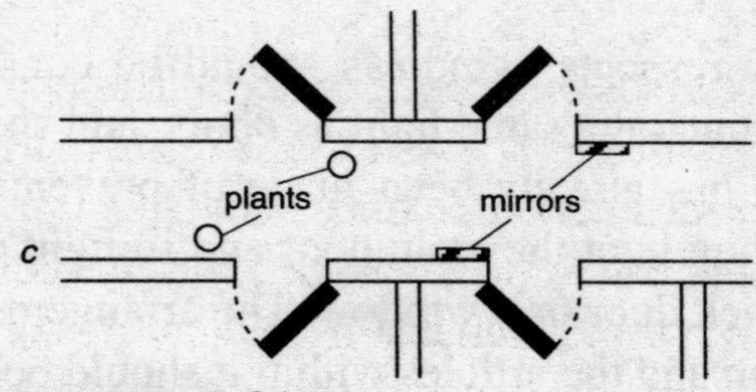

c

poor arrangement of doors

corridor, particularly if the corridor is long, is likely to suffer from sha chi and this can be corrected by fastening a long mirror to the side of the door facing the corridor.

It hardly needs stating because it is so obvious, but doors should be easy to open and should not be hindered in their opening by furniture inside the room. It is not always possible to arrange the furniture in a room precisely as required, but every effort should be made to provide easy access into the room. Later sections will concentrate upon how furniture can best be placed in rooms.

Dealing with windows

In many respects, windows should be considered in much the same light as doors, and some mention has already been made of preventing chi flowing in at the main door and straight out of the back door or a window. The arrangement of a room and the articles within it should be so as to promote the smooth flow of chi entering and leaving the room. To prevent the rapid loss of chi, should this be happening, we can to some extent refer to the remedies suggested already – such as covering the window with a curtain, even if the curtain is made only of lace.

A general principle is that windows (and doors) should not be sited near to the corner of a room as this enables the chi to move out of the room too quickly. If the eight points (mentioned earlier) are superimposed on the room, it will be seen in which category there will be a loss of chi and therefore a negative effect on one aspect of your life. If, for example the chi flows quickly through and out of the room as shown in figure 24 at the point where the area for children is situated, then one may expect some difficulties in that aspect of your personal life. This room clearly also has some negative features with regard to the friends aspect and the confining nature of the door. This will need some remedial action as it is better not to have doors or windows

Figure 24

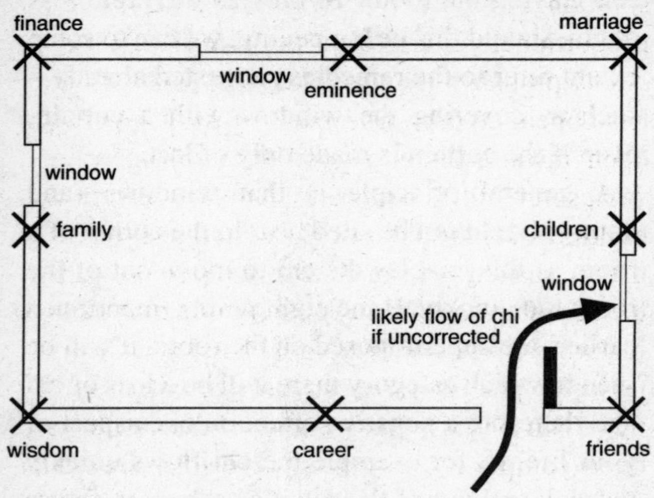

at the corners of rooms – in this case there is a danger of losing chi too rapidly in the area of friends.

To counteract the rapid exit of chi through the side window, a simple lace curtain and perhaps a small vase of flowers would provide the ideal solution. A relatively simple action can have a proportionately far greater positive effect.

It is probably the standard, but windows are best opening outwards but if they happen to open inwards, it is a good idea to determine what sort of chi is being admitted (*see* section on buildings). If the chi is negative and disruptive – that is, sha chi – it can be diverted or blocked by the use of a vase of flowers at the window, hanging wind chimes or something similar, or a strategically placed mirror if the configuration of the room permits this. Many windows do not open completely, either because they are sash windows where at most one half of the aperture is covered, or because they are modern UPVC double glazed units that have a fixed lower panel and an opening upper panel. In these cases it will help to place flowers at the lower closed part of the window.

The entrance hall, porch or foyer

Of course, there are many houses where entry is made directly from the street into a room. However, most buildings have an entrance hall of some description albeit rather small, and there is a tremendous variety in the nature of the entrance hall and the available space. Homes with a small room of this nature will clearly be a little more private and can be quieter than arrangements where there is no hall.

General principles are that a window in the hall is useful to ensure that the chi moves around – it is not good for the chi to become too static. It is not ideal to have the front door opening onto a small hall from which a staircase ascends. It is very likely that the chi in this situation will flow straight out of the door. It then becomes necessary to slow down the chi to prevent this happening and this can be accomplished by hanging wind chimes (*see* figure 25). It is not possible to use a mirror in this situation, but a plant set on a

Figure 25 – outside door opening onto stairs. Mirror can be used but of less significance.

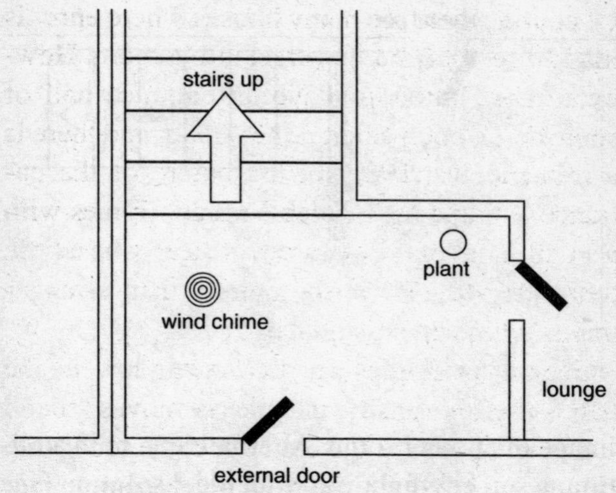

stand could also help matters. If the stairs are at an angle to the outside door, then a mirror can be used to divert the chi and also to provide a reflection of the interior of the house. It may be possible to position the mirror such that it reflects a nice view from another window, or an

Figure 26 – possible use of screen and mirror to prevent escape of chi. Wind chimes could also be added.

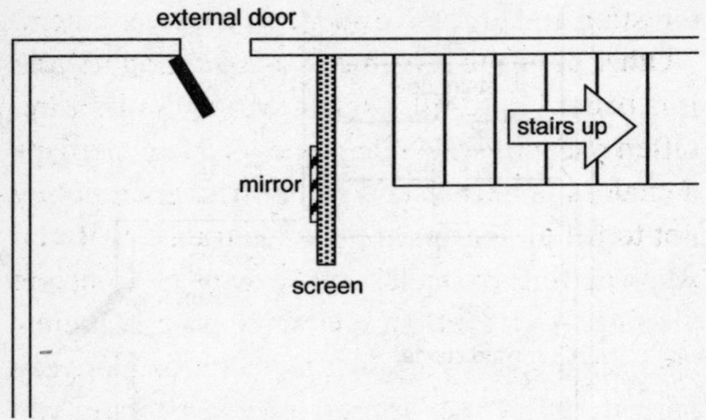

image of another room. Alternatively, or in addition, a screen might prove an ideal solution (*see* figure 26), providing a barrier to stop the escape of chi and enabling a mirror to be hung at an angle to the door thus providing a reflection of the inside.

It is not a good idea to place a mirror immediately opposite the outside door, such that anyone entering the house sees an image of themselves!

Far better would be to hang a picture or something similar on the facing wall to present an interesting and attractive scene to whoever enters.

Other points to remember about entrances are: it is better not to fill a small area with furniture. Often one will see a telephone on a tale, perhaps a chair, a bookcase and so on. It is good policy not to fill up the space by the entrance as if you were putting obstacles in the way of someone visiting. A clear, light and airy space is preferable. If the available space is very small, or very narrow, the overall impression can be improved dramatically through the adoption of a light colour-scheme and relatively soft lighting.

Entrances often open directly into corridors or long hallways or even a lobby type of space from which several doors lead to the other rooms. It has already been mentioned that a long corridor with many doors leading off is not ideal and the corridor tends to channel the chi, making it move too quickly. Corridors are the means whereby chi moves to each of the rooms. It is important that the chi does not move too quickly and that it is not obstructed by items of furniture in the corridor. When the corridors and other common spaces such as landings are clear then the building is more likely to be filled with good chi. However, if there is a lot of awkward furniture to be avoided and generally a jumble of other bits and pieces the flow of chi is affected adversely and this has a knock-on effect upon each of the rooms, making the building, overall, a less welcoming and healthy place in which to live.

When corridors are particularly narrow, they are susceptible to the production of sha chi. The remedy is to prevent the chi flowing so quickly and in a straight line and this is best done by placing mirrors on the walls which has the effect of creating a more wavy course for the chi. It has already been mentioned that hanging wind chimes or banners across the corridor will also help. The problems associated with corridors tend, in the main, to be found in commercial office buildings rather than domestic homes.

However, homes that do have an elongated design, particularly some one-storey buildings, may well have a long corridor that can be quite dark and stifling. Even so, there is much that can be done through the use of mirrors, wall hangings, subtle lighting and plants, providing space allows.

Very often the entrance hall, or a short corridor from the front door of a house, will lead first to the lounge or sitting room, and this is the room dealt with next.

The lounge

The lounge or living room, as the name suggests, is quite possibly the room where most time is spent and it is considered to be the room most yang in character. The bedroom and the kitchen, particularly if the latter is a dining kitchen, are also used a great deal but the lounge can be the most-shared room in the house. It not only serves as the gathering place for the family,

Figure 27

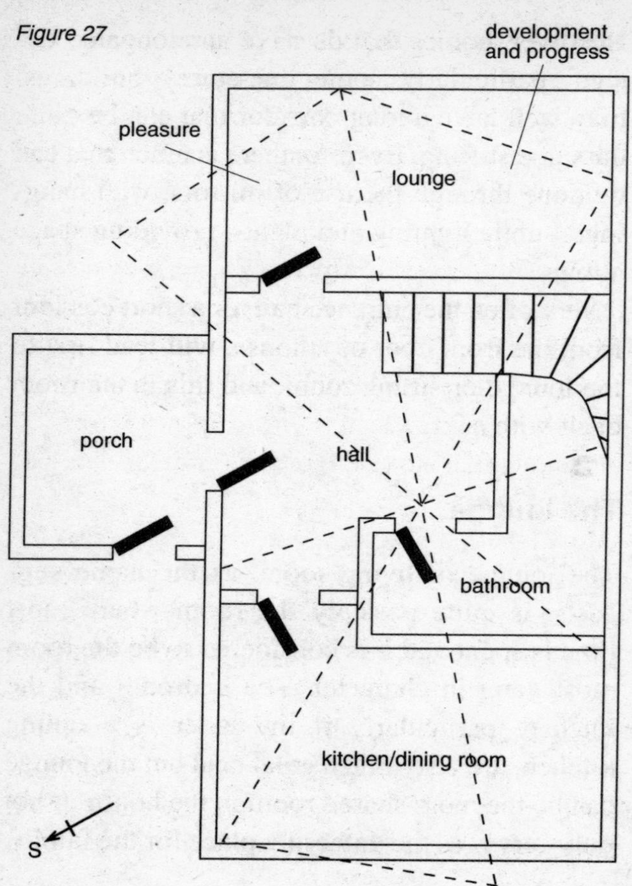
development
and progress
pleasure
lounge
porch
hall
bathroom
kitchen/dining room
S

whether watching television or just relaxing, but it is also the focal point for socialising when friends are invited in for an evening. It will therefore benefit from being comfortable and welcoming, warm and light without being too bright and glaring.

A preliminary assessment of the room can be made by laying the Pah Kwa over the ground plan of the house. Then it will be possible to see in which of the eight sectors the rooms is situated. The grid is placed facing south irrespective of the direction of facing of the house and the location of the lounge can then be determined. Figure 27 shows the Pah Kwa superimposed upon the ground-floor plan of a real house with the different areas partially drawn in. The main door faces south east hence this is taken as the direction of facing of the house. It is interesting to note that prior to the addition of the porch some years ago, the door that now forms the entrance into the hall, was the main door and it then faced south west which would have generated a different analysis.

In this instance, the lounge falls within the areas of pleasure, and development and progress. This is a reasonable combination and quite appropriate for a lounge. It means that it lends itself to entertaining, socialising, and potential, whether it be discussing new plans and ventures or just capitalising upon forthcoming opportunities. There are certain stipulations and rules that some practitioners attach to this procedure but because of the outline of your house or the direction relative to the south facing Pah Kwa, it is not always possible to be absolutely accurate. However, it is perfectly possible to get a general idea of the endowments that apply and the likely outcome. Ideally, the octagonal outline of the Pah Kwa should include two outside walls, the ones that are furthest apart, but this is not always feasible. However, the extent of the octagon will cut walls at certain points and this gives an indication of the endowments that a particular room lacks or has in excess. In this particular example, there are extra areas for both the pleasure and development endowments indicating strengths in these aspects and although there is part of the pleasure area missing, the prospects for this room and the occupiers is good.

When applying the eight points to this room, the configuration is quite straightforward due to the rectangular nature of the room (*see* figure 28). This means that no one aspect is exagger-

Figure 28

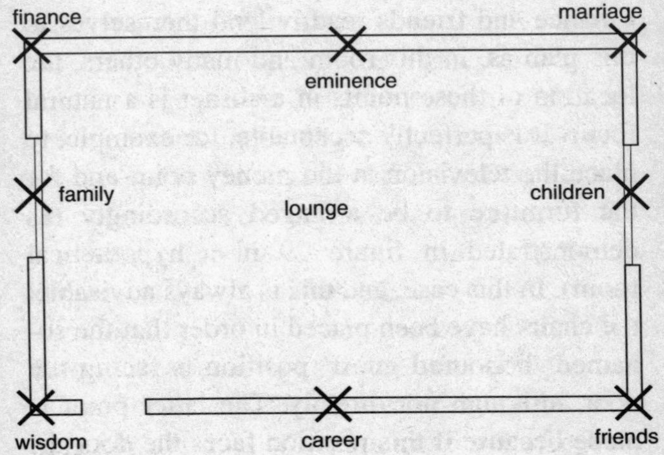

ated or diminished as would be indicated by a room extension or indentation.

One of the many ways in which Feng Shui can help in the home, in addition to the placement of mirrors, and so on, to assist the correct flow of chi, is through the arrangement of furniture. There are a number of principles that can be followed when arranging furniture in this room. It can be focused around one of the eight points, preferably finance, marriage or friends. Finance and friends readily lend themselves to this plan as, in this room and many others, the location of these points in a corner is a natural focus. It is perfectly acceptable, for example, to place the television at the money point and for the furniture to be arranged accordingly (as demonstrated in figure 29 in a hypothetical room). In this case, and this is always advisable, the chairs have been placed in order that the so-named 'honoured guest' position is facing the door, although not directly. The latter point is made because if this position faces the door directly it is rather confrontational and someone entering the room will face you, or your guest, directly rather than obliquely which leaves scope for choice in responses and movements. Note that the arrangement of furniture as shown here is well on the way to the octagonal configuration of Pah Kwa which is a natural and pleasing layout.

Figure 29

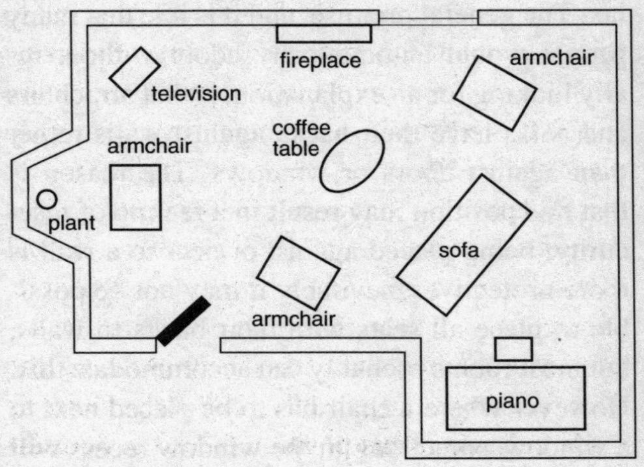

The honoured guest position is nevertheless considered to be the best in the room and is often near to the fire, if there is one, and it would probably face the television comfortably. It may also face towards a window with a nice view although it is better to have an oblique view out of the window – to be facing it directly may create a feeling of being too exposed. It is the place a guest would be offered and it is almost certainly the armchair in which you would choose to relax. The general premise, and it is one that many people would automatically adopt without really looking for an explanation, is that armchairs and sofas have their backs against walls rather than against doors or windows. The reason is that this position may result in a feeling of insecurity; being placed against or near to a wall is more protective. Inevitably it may not be possible to place all seats with their backs to walls, but most rooms probably can accommodate this. However where a chair has to be placed next to a window, something in the window recess will help, a plant or a set of low bookshelves perhaps.

There are, in addition, a number of possible placements for the chairs and sofas, relative to each other. If chairs are placed opposite each other, even over an intervening low table, this obviously creates the situation where people are face to face, which may be fine for those who want to talk earnestly to each other, but not so comfortable for those who hardly know each other or who are not conversationalists. There is nothing worse than being seated opposite a garrulous person when you do not feel like talking or responding in like manner. Thus if the chairs or sofas are at right angles to each other there is more comfort in this layout and a person at the end of one sofa can enter the conversation when he or she wishes. Similarly, if the sofa and chairs are arranged as shown in figure 29, basically with two chairs facing but at angles to the sofa, this is perhaps the configuration with which everyone can be happy. There is no need for directly facing another person and there is the option of directing comments to all or just one person.

If the room in question has a number of alcoves, for example on either side of a chimney breast, then these can be improved by placing plants in the space to help the flow of chi. Lights are also useful in this respect, particularly if placed in conjunction with a painting hung on the wall. As mentioned previously, a tank of fish is also considered very beneficial.

It is, however, important that a lounge does not become overfilled and therefore strewn with too many items of furniture, plants, ornaments and so on; the chi must be able to flow around quite easily otherwise a feeling of laziness and apathy will be created.

Many lounges are combined with a dining area in one room. It is preferable that on entering the lounge, the dining room/area is not visible. If it is a dining area at one end of the lounge, it should be relatively easy to create a screen and this can be turned into an attractive feature, perhaps with plants and pictures of some sort.

The dining room

Many of the general points mentioned for the lounge are also applicable to the dining room. The room should be arranged so that the chi can flow around easily and it should be made comfortable and familiar. Ideally the room should be enclosed but if, as discussed above, your house contains a combined lounge and dining room, then the dining area should be partitioned from the remainder of the room to create what is in effect a separate room. This can be achieved in an attractive fashion through the use of a wooden frame upon which plants can climb, and pictures and mirrors can be hung and through the placing of a unit of bookshelves or similar item of furniture. This creates the intimacy necessary and with a warm colour scheme, possibly different from the lounge itself, the overall feel will be very congenial. It helps to have cheerful pictures and a fresh, light scheme of decoration. Too many windows are considered a bad thing as they can cause uneasiness and distraction. However, these can remedied by the use of lace curtains or flowers as discussed previously. Whether the dining room is a separate room or a partitioned area, it should ideally have no more than two entrances.

The main item of furniture is, of course, the dining table and chairs. Although it is favourable for each chair to have its back to a wall, this is clearly not always going to be possible. Also, many would advocate placing an even number of chairs around the table as even numbers are considered very auspicious. This is probably due to the fact that pairs invariably conjure images of partnerships and love. However, if there are five members to your family, it is likely you will usually have an odd number of chairs around your dining table. Nevertheless, there

Figure 30 – dining room configuration

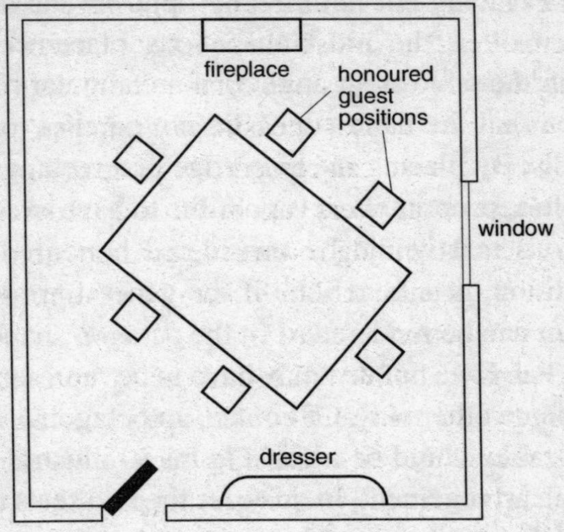

are certain positions and placements of furniture that will create the most beneficial layout and allow the chi to flow readily around the room.

It would be avoided anyway, but the door on opening should not clash with the back of a chair. There is also an honoured-guest position in the dining room as there is in the lounge, again facing but not directly opposite the door. Very often the most auspicious placement is with the table at an angle to a rectangular room such that the table edges are not parallel to the walls. By placing the long edge of a rectangular table appropriately, it is possible to have two positions that would be considered honoured. In addition, it is beneficial if the general arrangement can be rendered to fit the octagon shape of the Pah Kwa but this may have to be represented in some other way. Of course, an octagonal dining table would be ideal! Figure 30 illustrates a basic arrangement. In this case the two seats facing the door are in the honoured position, no chair has its back to the window, and although two seats are placed with their backs to the door, which is not an ideal set-up, there is an oblique view through the window. A slight modification is shown in figure 31, with the table rotated a little more. This means that the second honoured-guest position is now somewhat more distant,

Figure 31 – alternative configuration for the dining room

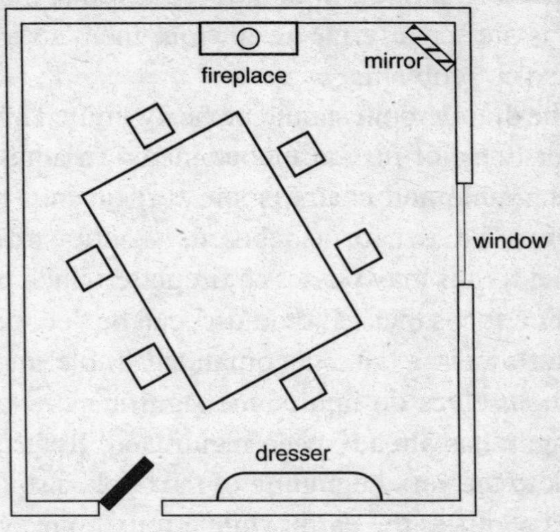

but still valid, but it does mean that no-one is sitting with their back directly to the door. Once again, there are additional, small touches that can be made such as a vase of flowers in the hearth of the fireplace and across the far corner of the room, either a mirror, decorative screen or something similar. In both these layouts, the table is sufficiently far away from them so as to cause no problem.

The dining room should be fairly limited in the other items of furniture contained – in addition to the table and chairs, some sort of unit, perhaps a dresser or sideboard, would suffice. Some rooms may possess a fireplace which provides a focus that, if not in use, can be decorated with flowers, a fan or an ornament. Table shapes in themselves do hold some significance – the octagon has already been mentioned. Referring back to the very beginning of the book, a square table signifies the earth while a round one symbolises heaven. Of all the tables available only the rectangle and the oval present a position for the head of the table and are therefore considered more formal than other shapes (circle, square, etc) where there is no place for the head. For equality in a large family, a circular table is clearly the most suitable!

The kitchen

The kitchen is likely to be one of the busiest rooms in the house. In many homes, in addition to its primary function, the kitchen forms the social focus for the family and callers and almost everything happens there, especially if it is combined with a dining area that is used for day-to-day meals.

Clearly this is the room where food is prepared and it therefore represents the life of the household. It needs to be a room that can easily accommodate people going to and fro and yet provide all the necessary facilities for preparation of food, in a bright and if possible spacious area. The ideal position of being able to see whoever enters the room is not always possible in a kitchen when working at the cooker, sink or a worktop. However, providing the walls are not all covered with fitted cupboards, mirrors can be hung to counteract this problem and these will have the added benefit of making the room

Figure 32 – encroachment into kitchen

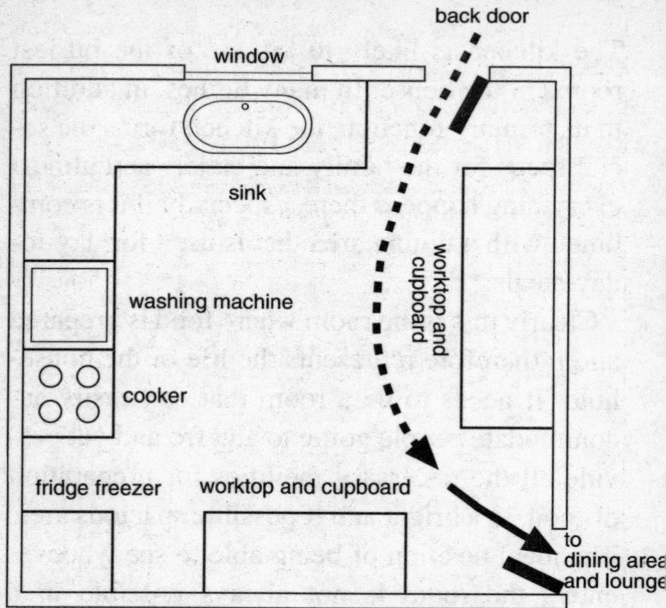

appear more spacious. The kitchen should not become a through way with constant traffic as this will disrupt anyone who is trying to work there. However, quite often and particularly in modern houses, the back door opens into the kitchen, so there is inevitably some conflict here. It may, however, be possible to create a passageway or walkway which helps to keep the kitchen self-contained (see figures 32 and 33).

Figure 33 – kitchen modification with improved flow and less disruption of the kitchen environment

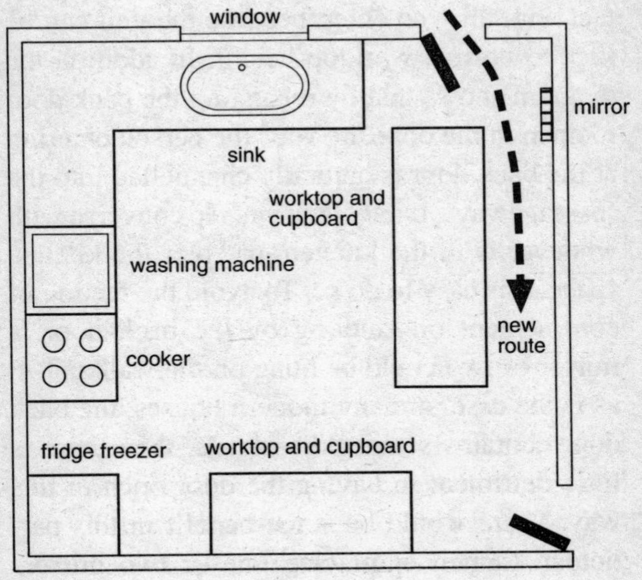

In figure 33, the kitchen cupboard/worktop unit has been moved to create a natural route for anyone wishing to move between the kitchen door and the door to the lounge, and vice versa. This simple alteration can readily be accomplished and creates the self-contained space for the person in the kitchen while maintaining contact with all who enter, because the unit can be kept to normal worktop height. In addition the diagram shows that by rehanging the back door to open in the opposite way, the person entering at the back door is naturally channelled into the 'passageway'. If they then wish to converse with whoever is in the kitchen, or enter the kitchen space, it is easy to do so. To avoid the feeling of confinement on entering by the back door, a mirror or two could be hung on the wall and if, as is the case in many modern houses, the back door contains some glass panels, then there is little detriment in having the door open in this way. There would be some benefit in this particular kitchen of placing one or two mirrors elsewhere notably above the washing machine and the unit on the same wall as the refrigerator/ freezer.

It is interesting to consider briefly the influence that the five elements might have on the layout of a kitchen such as this. The elements in question are water (for the sink and the refrigerator) and fire (for the cooker). As mentioned earlier, there is a conflict between these two elements and the moderating influence is wood. It is considered best to avoid having the cooker placed opposite or next to the sink and/or refrigerator as this generates sha chi. The likely negative effects may include agitation, an argumentative family life or poor financial prospects. Because wood acts as the moderator between these two elements, then the situation can be remedied by inserting something relating to wood, which in terms of colours is something blue or green. This could be wall or floor tiles of the appropriate colour placed between the appliances in question or an ornament of the same colour.

It is well worthwhile trying to improve the Feng Shui of the kitchen as this is a much-used room and it contributes greatly to the overall well-being of the house and its occupants, not least because it is where food is prepared! As such, the kitchen is at the heart of family life and eating together as a family is a natural and constructive progression.

Stairs

We have already mentioned some aspects regarding the location of stairs, in the section on the Entrance Hall. The main situation to avoid is stairs descending into the hall or that face the outer door directly leading to a loss of chi which suggests a loss of money. It will also result in the rooms on the upper floor becoming depleted. This can be remedied to some extent in the manner discussed, with wind chimes, screens, mirrors and so on. Stairs that curve are good when it comes to the flow of chi and if the stairs curve

Figure 34 – good layout of stairs for the flow of chi

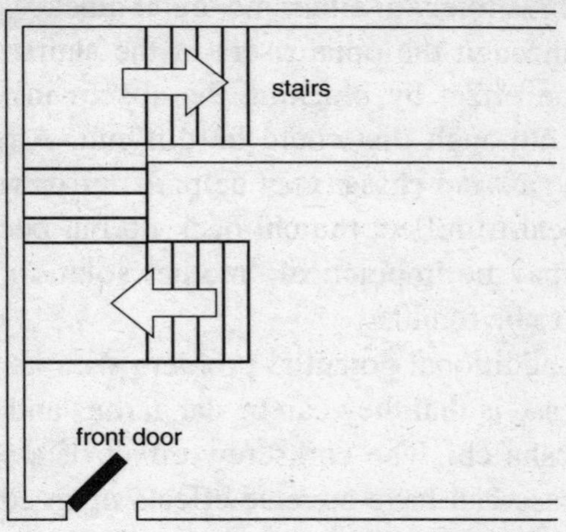

away from the door towards the foot then this will prevent loss of chi (*see* figure 34). In this illustration the stairs turn at right angles at two landings. The same effect can be accomplished equally well with continuously curving stairs. However, it should be mentioned that a spiral staircase is not necessarily the very good thing that it might at first seem to be. In this instance, the chi is likely to either move too quickly or be lost through the open risers in the stairs. This can be offset by blocking the spaces in some way, although this could be difficult. Alternatively, a wind chime may help. A mirror would be ideal to reflect the chi back up but because this may be impractical, another solution may have to be found.

An additional potential problem with a spiral staircase is that they can be dangerous and generate sha chi. The corkscrew effect of a spiral staircase can have adverse effects upon certain aspects of your life. This can be offset by placing plants and lights beneath the staircase.

The bedroom

This is clearly a very important room as we all spend a considerable amount of time here! It is also the most intimate of rooms and should be laid out and decorated in such a manner so as to

The fundamental rule is to avoid the bed being placed with its foot directly opposite the door (*see* figure 35). This particular position has connotations of death because in China this is the way, traditionally, that a dead person is laid out and the corpse is taken from the room feet first. However, it is preferable to see who is entering the room so in this case the bed could be moved to a side wall or placed across a corner. Figure 36 shows some other options, all of which would be satisfactory.

Of the four positions outlined in figure 36, the oblique configuration across the corner, shown by the dashed line, may need something placed at the foot of the bed. This is because it is preferable to avoid chi flowing in through the door and straight over the bed as this can disturb sleep. Although the position in question does not allow direct flow of chi over the bed, a screen or plant placed at the foot will help. In any event, there are enough options in this room, but this remedy can be adopted where the options are limited.

Figure 36 – possibilities for positioning the bed in a bedroom

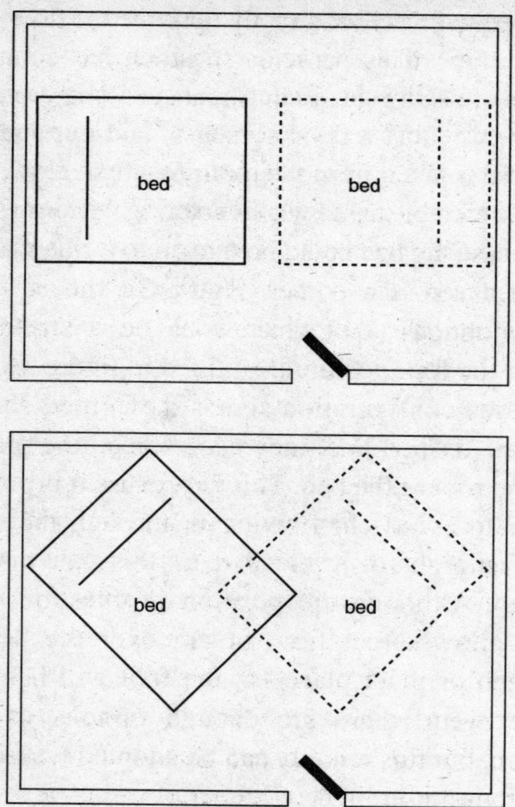

Other configurations to avoid are with the foot of the bed directed to a window or with the bed head beneath a window. Furthermore, it is preferable to allow adequate space on the three sides of the bed for easy access. This assumes of course that a couple is sharing the bed.

Bedrooms contain other items of furniture: chairs, dressing table, wardrobes, sets of drawers, and so on. It is advisable to avoid overcrowding the room and to place these other items to complement the position of the bed. As mentioned, the atmosphere should be calm and since mirrors tend to stimulate chi, too many mirrors would be a bad thing. A dressing table usually has a mirror attached, and if placed sensibly, for example across a corner, it can work constructively in maintaining the steady flow of chi. A second mirror on the wall would be acceptable but there is little need for more. If another mirror is required then it can be placed on the inside of a wardrobe door and used only when necessary. It is generally considered to

Figure 37 – arrangement of furniture in a bedroom

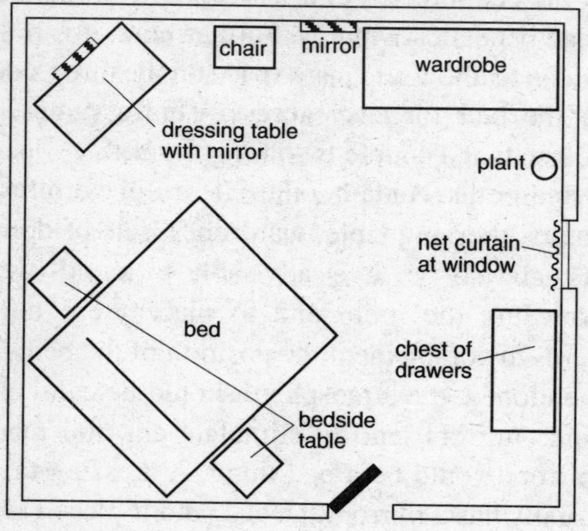

create a disturbing effect if a mirror is positioned so as to allow you to see yourself in bed. Whatever other pieces of furniture are placed in the room, avoid aligning them in a way that leaves sharp edges directed towards the bed. Figure 37 shows a satisfactory arrangement taking into account the typical items of furniture to be included and the likely layout of a standard room. In this case the bed and dressing table are placed across two corners. This is only a practical solution if the room is sufficiently large, and in this instance the wardrobe could also have been placed across the third corner. This would be quite a good arrangement because the general layout would then have approached the octago-

Figure 38 – layout for a small bedroom

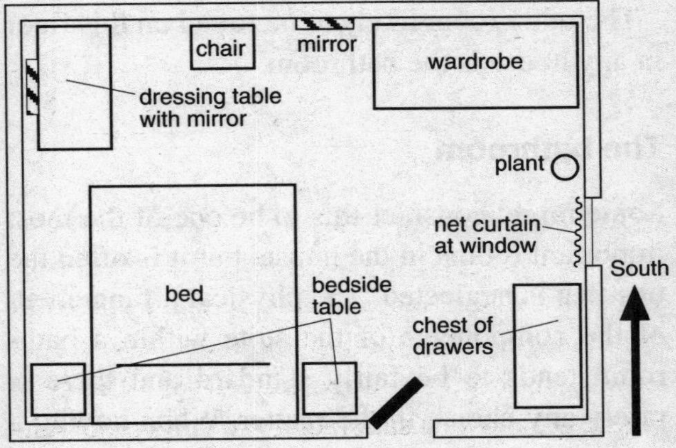

nal shape of the Pah Kwa. Also seen in figure 37 is the plant between the wardrobe and window. This both moderates the flow of chi and generates positive chi. A smaller room in which these three items (bed, dressing table and wardrobe) were flat against the wall would have worked perfectly well (*see* figure 38). If the octagonal arrangement of the eight endowments is placed over this room it can be seen that the bed falls within the family/harmonious areas which is also good.

The other room likely to be found on this floor in any house is the bathroom.

The bathroom

Some might consider this to be one of the most important rooms in the house, but it is often the one that is neglected. The physical arrangement of the components of the suite within a bathroom tends to be fairly standard and there is rarely any choice in the matter. When buying a house, the last thing you will want to do, unless this is in your plans anyway, is to completely re-arrange the bathroom. However, the application of some basic principles will help.

The same guidelines apply here as in other rooms – whatever you may be doing, ensure that you can see anyone who may come in to the room. Now of course it is not generally very likely that someone will enter the bathroom if you are already in there taking a bath, a shower, or sitting on the toilet! Nevertheless, the same

Figure 39 – arranging the bathroom optimally

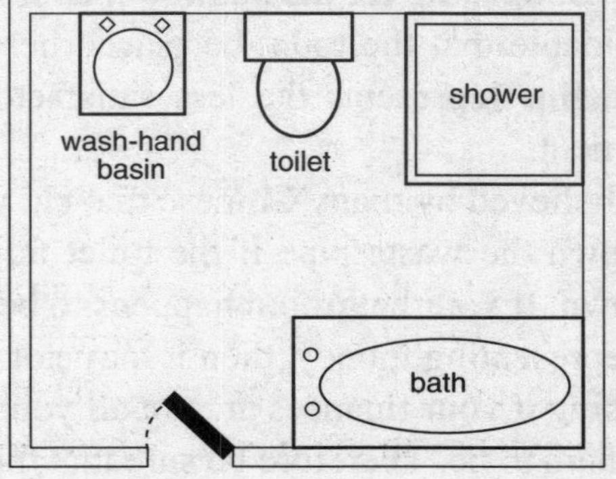

principles apply – be positioned so that you can see everything from your position, which should be the best position in the room. This means that each item of bathroom furniture should be positioned so that the person using it does not have his/her back to the door (*see* figure 39). Certainly the toilet should not be the first piece of the bathroom suite seen on entering the room! In any event, it is customary practice when fitting a bathroom to avoid this situation and to have the door opening so as to 'cover' the toilet and not to expose it. Figure 40 shows the preferred direction of opening for the bathroom door (if it is unavoidable that the toilet be placed here); the dashed line represents the less satisfactory arrangement.

It is believed by many Chinese that chi will be lost down the waste pipe if the toilet lid is not put down. If your bathroom happens to be in the area representing money, then it may not be too surprising if your finances are not all you would wish them to be. Therefore be sure that the lid is

Figure 40 – door opening for a bathroom

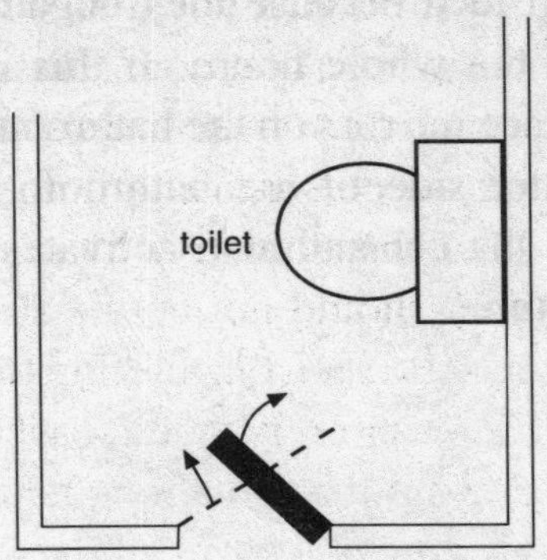

always down and it also helps to keep the bathroom door closed.

The location of the bathroom is also considered by some to be important. It is preferable not to have the bathroom situated in the west or north east of the house plan. If this is the case however, it is good policy to decorate the room accordingly – earth colours of yellow, ochre, etc, for the former and all white for the latter.

Also, bathrooms at the centre of the house are not a good idea because they negatively affect the chi of the whole house. If this is the case, you can place mirrors on the bathroom walls and on the outer side of the bathroom door. This keeps out sha chi and also activates chi inside the bathroom.

Applying Feng Shui to Building Exteriors

When contemplating moving house, the opportunity arises to apply Feng Shui in a beneficial way, in much the same way as we improve a house through interior design and decoration. The location and direction of facing is relevant, as is the type of structure in which you live. If a move is not imminent, then it is worth considering anyway, so that remedies can be applied wherever possible.

Looking around you

Depending upon the direction, there will be a different type of chi trained upon your home. It is necessary to look around your immediate area to see whether there is good or bad Feng Shui. There may be four types of chi involved: yang chi from the south; t'sang chi from the north; sheng chi from the east, and sha chi from the west.

As we already know sha chi is disruptive, so it is important to see whether there is any way in which it can enter the west-facing doors and windows of your house. If there is some possibility of this happening when they are open, then countermeasures must be employed, such as a mirror opposite the door if the main door is on the west. This will reflect back out the sha chi. Also, windows on the west side of the house can be susceptible so chimes or similar hanging ornaments will help, as will plants.

The remaining types of chi are more helpful and creative: sheng chi provides creative energy; from the north comes t'sang chi or hidden chi which induces relaxation and sleep; and from the south is yang chi which is nourishing.

Building types and environments

Although many people do not have much choice as to where they live, and this could also be said of those who are homeowners because there are always limitations to the houses in which we live, it is useful to know what to look out for so that some attempt can be made to remedy sha chi, for example.

Ordinary houses, whether detached or semi-detached have, to some extent, been mentioned elsewhere and aspects of Feng Shui concerning gardens will be dealt with in later sections. However, in certain buildings, there are additional points to consider. For example, living in a block of flats means there is chi coming up into your home and this may require you to take corrective measures. Even a two-storey building can have its complications, particularly if you live over certain retail establishments. It is not difficult to think of shops above which you would be happy or unhappy to live. Compare for example an undertaker's premises with a flower shop, or a betting shop with a bank. There are obvious differences and the chi will vary accordingly.

For a house in a terrace, it is necessary to

consider the chi from outside (front and back, whatever the directions may be) and also the chi from neighbours on both sides. In a basement flat the same sort of factors have to be considered, and it may be wise to consider exactly what sort of surroundings you may be moving into, in addition to the physical structure of the house or flat.

The immediate surroundings

There is much about Feng Shui that is very obvious and it is quite easy to assess a building and its location. Clearly a house in an industrial centre is not going to be as desirable as a pleasant semi-detached home on a new site next to fields, or a cottage set amongst woods, and so on. Most people will benefit from living in or near to countryside where there is fresh air, attractive views, trees and greenery and perhaps a stream or a lake. Conversely, living in a busy city with noise and vehicle exhaust pollution, possibly run-down buildings and certain inner-city problems will be subject to much sha chi and a great deal of effort will be necessary to remedy this situation. Much depends on the age of the individual person as the city may appeal to the younger generation, at least for a time. However, it is often the case that at some point we all would like to have a more peaceful environment.

Water is a very useful element to have around us as it has a soothing effect and it also carries chi. It is preferable to have a modest stretch of water – a small stream or pond – rather than a vast lake or a large man-made canal. This is because the best form of chi moves at a modest pace and does not travel in straight lines. This type of chi is associated with streams and smaller bodies of water. Conversely, sha chi travels in straight lines and is more likely to be generated by a canal than a stream. Also, a large body of water may be too oppressive for some as it builds up chi and if it were to your west it may build up sha chi. Also, as mentioned at the outset (*see also* figure 1) it is not good to have water, such as a river, flowing straight towards your house.

Water is, however, vital and if it is absent outside, then it can be provided indoors through the use of an aquarium, or perhaps a small fountain in a conservatory.

Trees are also important and they complement the buildings, the latter being considered as the yang element in the immediate surroundings while the trees are the yin element. There has to be a balance between these different aspects and a useful guideline is to have 40% yin and 60% yang in your surroundings. This means that buildings and hills (the yang part) can occupy three fifths while trees and hollows in the land take up two fifths. Trees provide a balancing factor for the buildings and the hills and are clearly, therefore, very important. Further aspects of the use of trees will be considered in the next section which deals with gardens.

Designing your Garden to Benefit from Feng Shui

It is very easy to concentrate so much upon the interior decor of your house that the garden is ignored; or perhaps you simply can't stand gardening anyway. Applying Feng Shui to the garden introduces a new perspective and one which is both interesting and productive.

As a general principle, and this is hardly surprising, the garden should complement the house. However, there is more to it than this simple generalisation. Houses are, in the main, angular constructions and there are many hard lines and sharp corners to them. The garden provides the opportunity to balance these hard edges with flowing shapes and gentle curved lines. If space permits, paths, flower beds, lawns

Figure 41 – garden layout before applying Feng Shui principles, illustrating the regimentation and hard edges

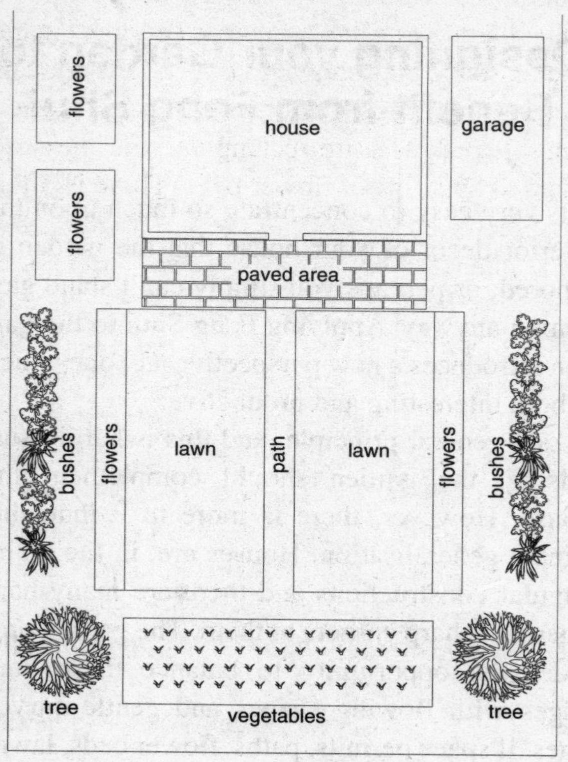

and ponds can all be used to enhance the Feng Shui of your garden.

It is therefore best to avoid hard outlines in the garden, so the plan shown in figure 41 is not particularly uplifting. It follows the pattern often seen where lawns are rectangular and they are bounded by strips of flower beds. There is often a symmetry about gardens, with a central path and similar features on either side of the path. In China, the tendency is, where there is space to make it possible, to opt for curved paths, rounded beds and grassed areas. Also special features are developed and these may be placed around a corner and half-hidden so that it is a pleasant surprise to come across a new view or area of the garden. This might be a fountain or a garden seat partially enclosed by a trellis and climbing plants, or perhaps an arbour, both of which provide a quiet corner. The scope is really quite considerable. Figure 42 shows one possibility for a rearranged garden based upon the site available in figure 41.

Figure 42 – the garden after the application of Feng Shui principles, with more rounded features and introduction of water

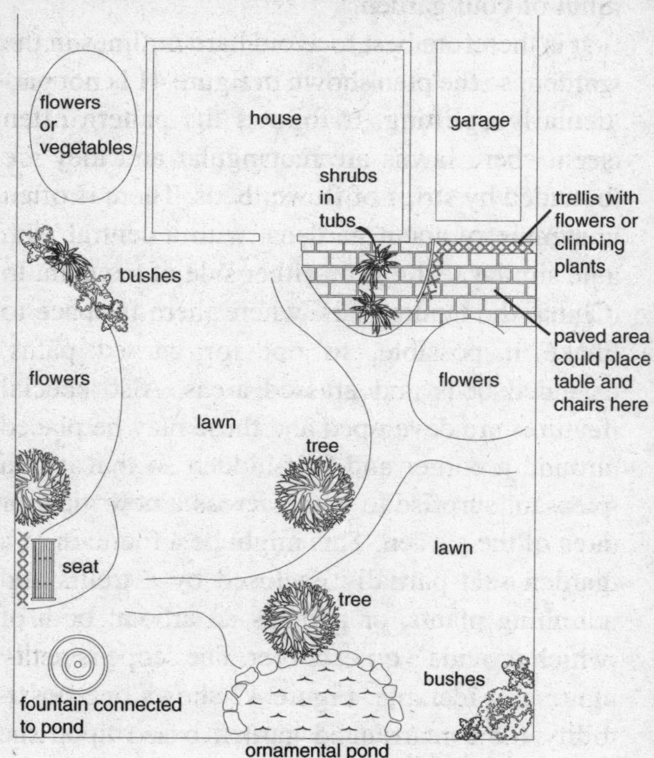

In the new layout, the major changes involve removing all traces of rectangular, regimented flower beds and lawns. All the components are still there but with more flowing outlines and, in addition, a fountain and pond have been at the end of the garden, providing the beneficial effects of water, but also a pleasant scene to be viewed from the garden seat. Next to the house, a paved area is retained but it is softened by use of shrubs in tubs. The placing of a trellis enhances this end of the garden in two ways. It cuts off the back wall of the garage, which is never a pretty sight and it provides a nice enclosed area in which a table and chairs can be sited. This allows a pleasant view of the rest of the garden and it also helps block off any immediate view of the house creating a feeling of peacefulness and solitude. This design dispenses almost completely with the small vegetable garden although a bed has been retained next to the house. It would, however, be perfectly feasible to have more ground devoted to vegetables.

Figure 43 – actual garden site for a terraced house

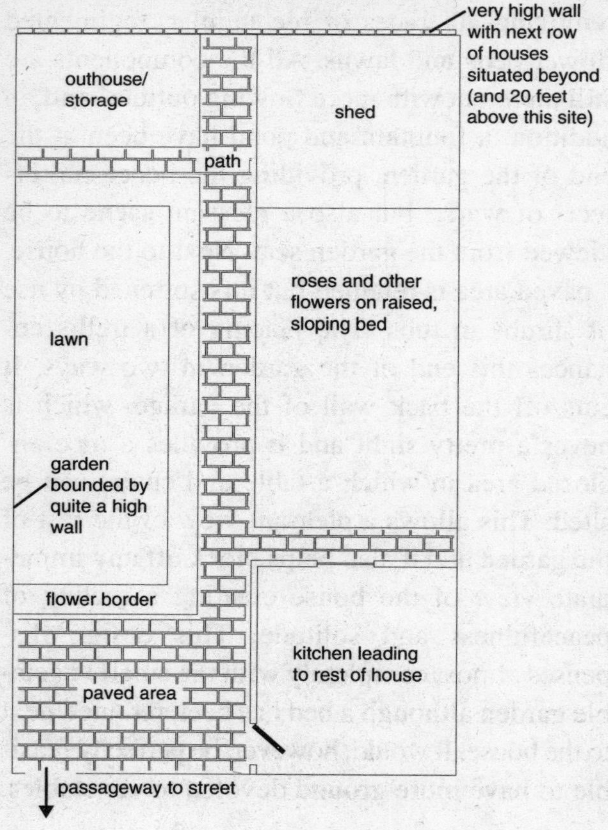

This could be partially screened from the rest of the garden by a hedge of some description and approached through a flowered arch (using, for example, clematis or honeysuckle). The scope is enormous.

It is fair to say that this is quite a large garden and many modern houses have very much less and some may have just a small yard. Even so, by applying the same principles a great deal can be achieved. Figure 43 shows the garden at the back of a terraced house – the garden is long and thin and is approached from a tunnel-like passage from the street. The door into the kitchen is effectively the back door of the house. Although the scope in terms of space is limited, much can still be done and figure 44 shows one possibility. This layout provides a much more inviting scene when entering the garden area from the passage and much more could be done.

Some of the individual features and aspects of the garden are now mentioned beginning with drives and paths.

Figure 44 – the garden site of Figure 43 modified by applying Feng Shui

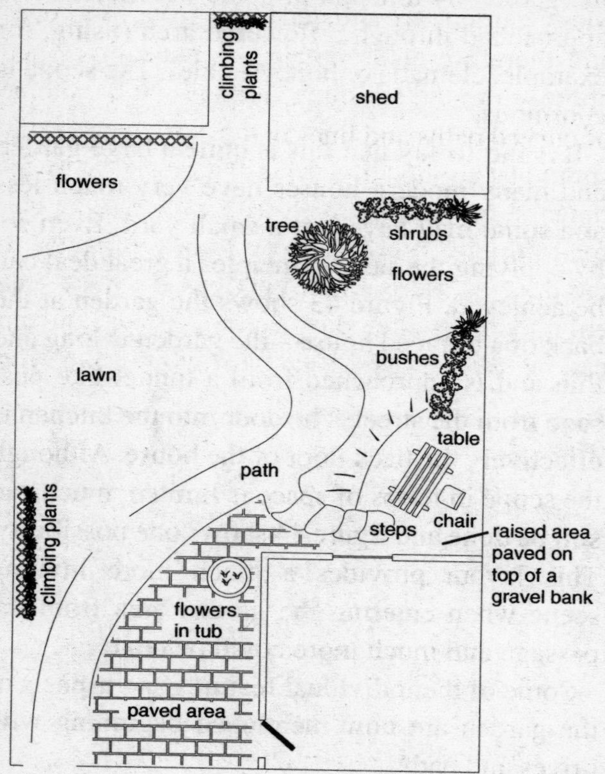

Drives and garden paths

Many gardens are situated to the front of a house and therefore also contain the main drive and approach to the building. In line with the theme of curved paths and lines in the garden, the same should be applied to a drive. There are many arrangements that adversely affect the flow of chi, for example, straight drives leading directly to the door or a drive narrowing to the door. Sha chi may be generated by a straight drive and chi can be concentrated by a narrowing drive. Too

Figure 45 – preferable configurations for drives/paths to the house

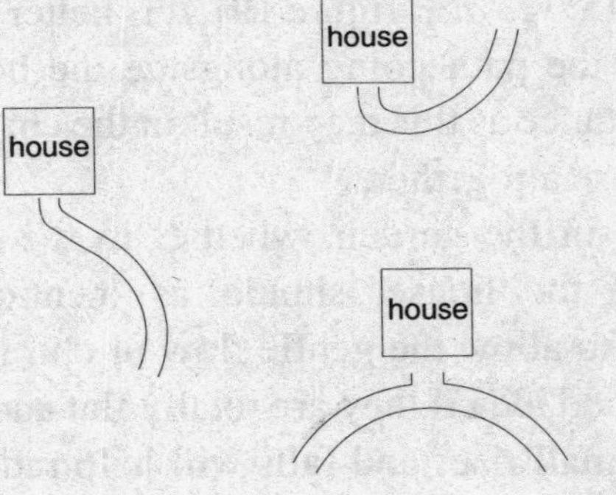

narrow a path will limit the flow of chi. As a general rule, however, a path or drive that has dimensions in keeping with the rest of the house should be fine. Much of course depends on the direction from which the chi originates and probably the best direction is south to south-east from which the beneficial yang and sheng chi come (giving a developing and sustaining influence).

In addition, and as stated elsewhere, the drive should not be positioned so that it runs directly up to the door. It is far better to have a curved drive or path, perhaps sloping away gently (*see* figure 45; *see also* figure 19). It is better to avoid having the path going alongside the house for any distance as this may result in the chi missing the house altogether.

Paths in the garden, whether to the front or rear of the house, should as mentioned be curved to allow the gentle flow of chi. It is also not a good idea if they are totally flat and level – a few small rises and falls will help reduce any sha chi. This is less important if the path or drive runs from the south, but the implication here is that a back garden path running from the south serves a north facing house which itself would need attention!

Trees in gardens

In most cases, it is better to have trees that present a rounded profile which blend in with the rest of the garden. As such, tall spiky conifers and firs are not usually a good idea, unless you live in a very mountainous area. The trees that best fit include willow, maple, magnolia, cherry and similar species.

If you move to a new house where there is a number of established trees, it is preferable, if at all possible, to leave the older, mature trees where they are. It is not good Feng Shui to chop down such a tree. The exception of course is when a tree or large shrub is dead or dying, or diseased. In this case it is perfectly acceptable to remove it, and it is recommended that you do so, particularly if the tree or shrub is in the front garden. Roses are also considered by some to be a bad idea as bushes with thorns are not recommended.

Water in the garden

Water is considered to be very important by the Chinese and it is thought to be vital to a garden as it helps the chi to move about and to stay within the garden. That is why many suggestions relating to the layout of gardens will include a fountain and/or a pond, if space permits. Fortunately it is possible to install a fountain in even a small garden at relatively little cost.

Patterns of water flow

In one of the ancient books relating to Feng Shui, the many different configurations that a body of water might adopt, with reference to a building, were listed as an aid in deciding where to build near water. The way in which the water flowed towards or flowed by a building would

Figure 46 – the ideal juxtaposition of house and water

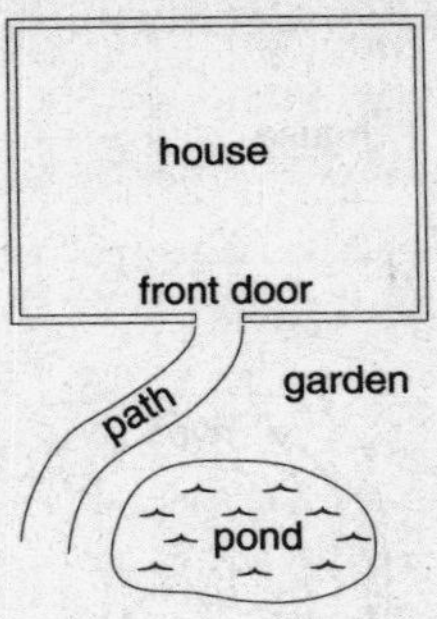

have significance. One of the ideal situations is to have water in front of your house (*see* figure 46) which could be a pond. Water flowing towards a house can have good and bad effects, depending upon its line of approach. If, as mentioned elsewhere in this book, the water flows directly at the house (*see* figure 47), then this brings sha chi to the house. If however, the water flows obliquely towards the house (*see* figure 48), in effect flowing past at an angle, this is quite favourable and is thought to bring financial success.

Figure 47 – this location is ill advised

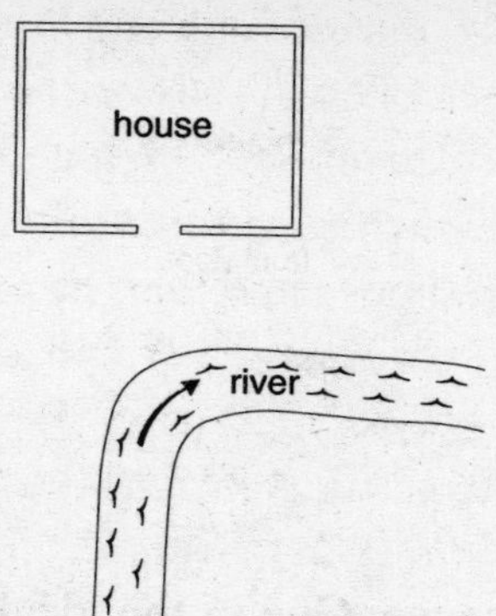

Figure 48 – the favourable configuration of water flowing towards, and past, a house

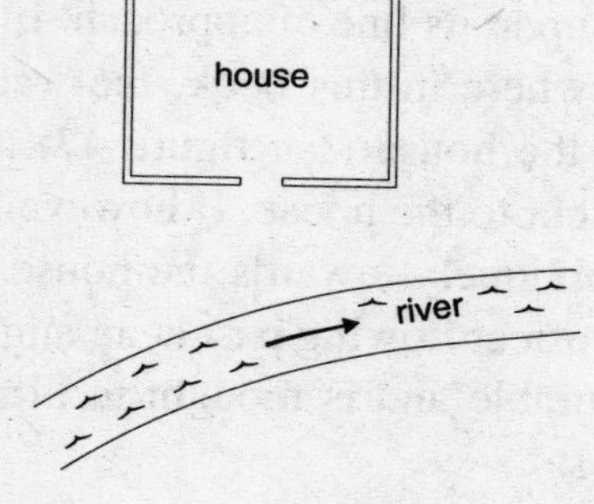

When the water flows past a house, it takes away the things that are bad and it is considered beneficial if the river or stream is then hidden from view as it leaves the location. Another beneficial arrangement is if the water flows along the front of the house and then turns to the side. There are two variations depending upon direction and orientation (*see* figures 49 and 50). The opposite, water turning away from a building, is not favourable. A pool in front of a house, which nevertheless is part of a river or stream flowing past in a favourable way, is also very beneficial as it represents the accumulation of wealth.

Figure 49 – a beneficial arrangement where the stream or river is said to 'embrace' the house

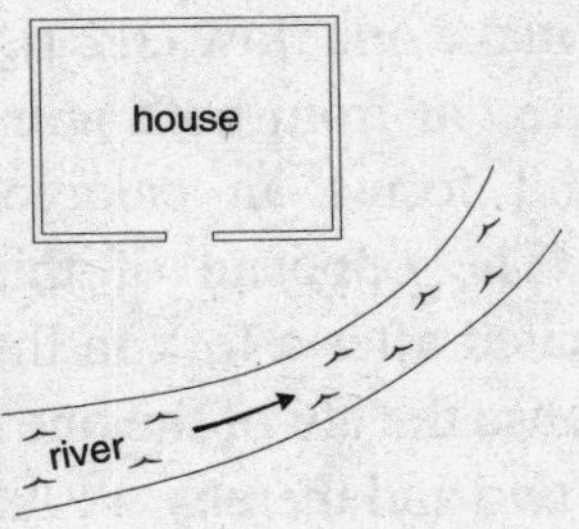

Figure 50 – this arrangement is considered very favourable indeed, as it can confer good luck on the house

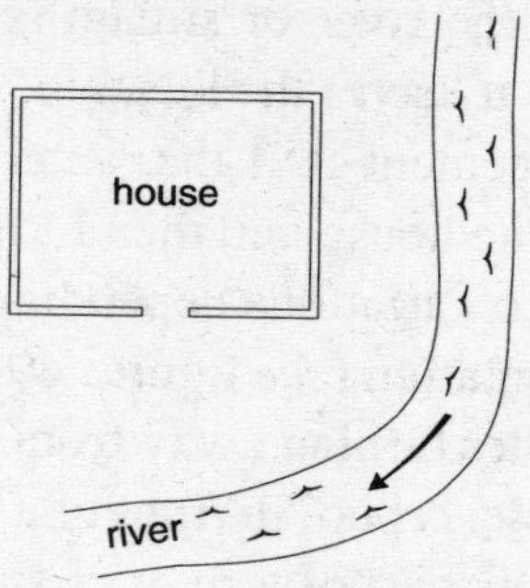

Also, because flowing water carries beneficial chi, it is very good for a house to be situated just beyond the point in a river where two tributaries converge to make one flow (*see* figure 51). This is because the chi from both arms of the river combines and forms an enlarged flow with greater chi. The opposite of this, where the house is situated after a fork in the river, is not so good because the chi of the one river is being divided into two and thereby weakened.

Figure 51 – a highly beneficial situation at the convergence of two streams or rivers

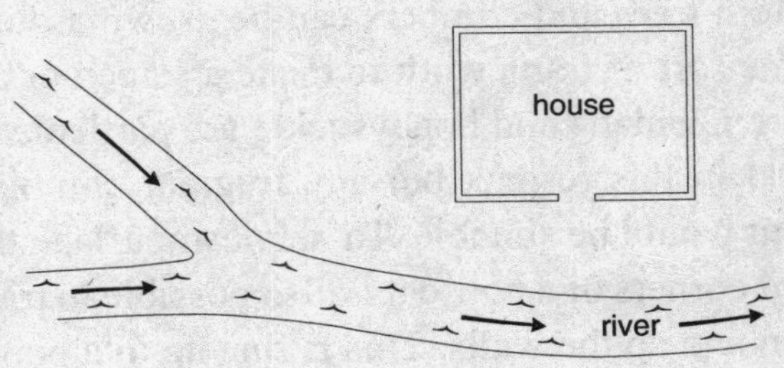

Hedges, shrubs and climbers

Hedges are very useful in gardens to help mark out areas without the use of harsh lines as created by fences or stones. It is also possible to make little corners and quiet areas with the use of hedges although it may take some planning and time to fully achieve your aim. It is preferable to select hedges with a natural look such as beech rather than trimming hedges such as privet to a hard-edged box-like barrier. In keeping with the general principles outlined, hedges should not be set out in straight lines but in gentle curves, if at all possible.

Both trees and climbers can be grown around some sort of framework to make a screen or arbour. Clematis and honeysuckle are particularly good in this respect but any fragrant climbing plant would be suitable. To help camouflage the hard corners of a house it is also possible to train climbers up the walls. This is fine up to a point, but it is important that it is kept under control and that the fabric of the house is not allowed to suffer as a result.

The use of paving stones

Areas covered with paving stones or slabs of some description can look very nice – they can also look rather sterile. It is therefore important to plan carefully where to place this area and precisely how it is to be laid out. It will probably be near the house, or if there are two, one can be nearer the house. In figure 42, a second paved area could be placed at the bottom left of the garden next to the fountain area. This could be surrounded with plants, bushes and climbers on an trellis to create an arbour-like corner.

As with many other aspects of Feng Shui, it is better not to have too regular an arrangement so if square slabs are used (say 2 feet square), try to avoid a regular pattern. An offset will help, or if smaller units are used a more intricate arrangement may be possible. Concrete paving stones are now available in many different shapes which can be used to good effect. In addition bricks can be used to create patterns, such as herringbone. Flagstones are ideal for paved areas as they have a natural appearance that blends in well with plants and the outlines of individual flagstones are randomly shaped.

In addition to considering the shape and arrangement of paving stones, other elements to take into account are what plants/shrubs might be used and should they be in pots and tubs or in gaps in the paving. This gives plenty of flexibility and ensures that any sha chi is broken up – it is the plain straight lines that perpetuate sha chi.

In addition, the careful placing of plants that have fragrant flowers will help the flow of chi and hinder the sha chi. The latter will be found where the smell is not so pleasant so it is worth bearing in mind when choosing the location for your dustbin. Ideally, the bin should be partially enclosed to keep it hidden. This can be achieved with an attractive fence and plants, shrubs suitably arranged.

Flowers

Flowers, particularly those with an attractive fragrance, will grace anywhere, whether growing in the garden or indoors in pots. Pleasant fragrances are very important in Feng Shui and those flowers with especially nice smells are ideal. Commonly used for their smell are honeysuckle, lilac, jasmine and buddleia. In addition, certain flowers are good for chi, among them lotus, lavender, sweet peas and lilies.

Symbolic meaning of flowers

The Chinese, and indeed other cultures, attribute significance and meaning to quite a number of flowers – we are all familiar with the symbol of romance and love as represented by the red rose. On a more light-hearted note, mistletoe means kiss me (and other emotions – *see* below). The following list provides examples, by no means exhaustive, of flower meanings.

Flower	**Meaning/Representation**
Acacia	hidden love
Amaryllis	pride
Anemone	sincerity
Aster	love
Azalea	womanhood, fragile, also 'Look after yourself for me'

Begonia	be careful
Bittersweet	truth
Bluebell	humility
bunch of dead flowers	rejected love
Camellia	admiration
Candytuft	indifference
Carnation	fascination; also admiration (red), innocence (white), rejection (yellow), I'll never forget you (pink)
Chrysanthemum	love (red) and truth (white)
Crocus	cheerfulness
Cyclamen	farewells
Daffodil	respect, 'You are the one'
Daisy	purity

Dandelion	happiness and devotion
Forget-me-not	true love
Forsythia	expectation
Freesia	faith
Geranium	stupidity
Gladioli	professing sincerity
Grass	surrender
Heather	admiration, fulfilled wishes (white)
Holly	happiness at home
Hyacinth	jealousy (yellow), regret and contrition (purple), constant (blue)
Hydrangea	insensitive
Iris	hope and trust, promise
Ivy	affection, friendship
Lilac	beauty

Lily	purity (white), gratefulness (yellow)
Lily of the valley	humility
Magnolia	dignity
Marigold	jealousy
Mistletoe	kiss me, overcoming difficulties, affection
Myrtle	love
Narcissus	correctness
Orchid	refinement, beauty
Pansy	happiness
Peony	compassion
Petunia	anger and bitterness
Poppy	oblivion, also consolation (white), success (yellow) and pleasure (red)
Primrose	I need you

Rhododendron	take care
Rose	love and romance (red), purity (white), jealousy (yellow), oneness (red and white), love at first sight (without thorns), grieving (dark red)
Snapdragon	deceit
Stock	loving ties
Sweet pea	leaving, thank you
Tulip	good luck, also I love you (red), warm smile (yellow)
Violet	virtue and faithfulness
Wallflower	faithfulness, particularly through bad times

The Use of Feng Shui for Business

Feng Shui can be applied to one's business whether the site is an office in a room at home or a separate building in the city. Much of what has already been described will apply to the office at home, but this topic will be dealt with shortly. Firstly let us consider business premises and their location and the internal arrangements.

The office building

It is often the case that the Chinese will, when deciding where to establish a business, consider the Feng Shui of the building and also wish to know a lot about it. Although in the west we would wish to have our office in as pleasant a location as possible – it's only natural – in China it is particularly important.

It is important that the shop or office is in an area that is busy and where there is good trade. It may also be important that the street is clean and inviting, otherwise passing trade may be deterred. However, it is not only these essentially superficial factors that are considered, but also the history of the site and shop premises. If the shop has changed hands numerous times and few if any businesses have made a success of their tenancy, then it might be wise to think again and find a more inviting location. If on the other hand, the shop is only available for good reasons, then it may present a better prospect. Perhaps someone is moving on because they have made such a success of their venture that despite their happiness with the current location, they must move to larger premises. This sort of location would seem very auspicious and in the eye of the customers, some of the positive aspects of the previous owner would inevitably make them consider the new business favourably and be willing to give it a try. These are all

Figure 52 – bad office sites

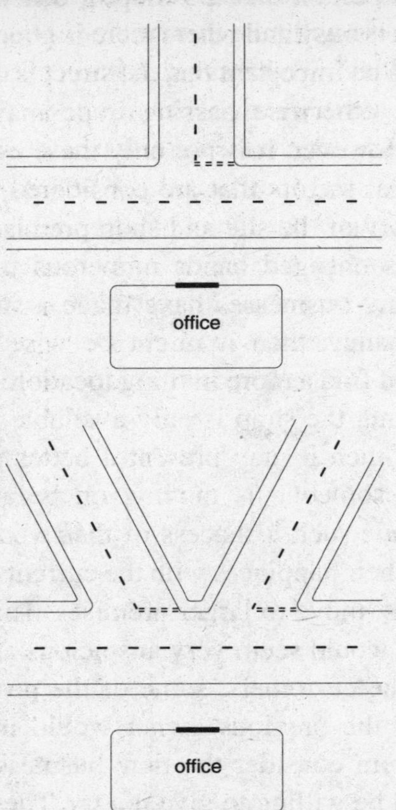

important aspects of the fuller picture. However, the Chinese will take this further in that, for example, they would avoid locating a business near to anything that has a connection with death, such as an undertaker's or a graveyard.

The physical location of the building is very important, and the factors that affect houses are also important for offices. For example, there should not be a road or roads aligned opposite the building as this will be a channel for too much chi. The chi moves more quickly than it

Figure 53 – good office sites

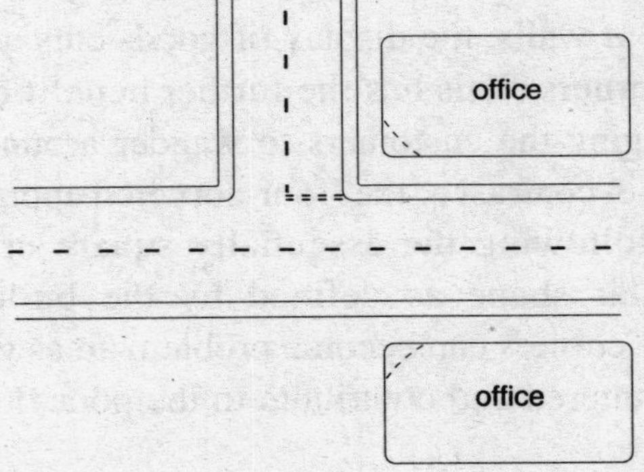

should and is often called 'killing chi'. Figure 52 shows bad configurations of roads and buildings while figure 53 illustrates better layouts. The 'vee' arrangement in figure 52 is especially bad because the chi is directed and funnelled towards your office. In addition to avoiding roads pointing at your building, it is better not to face the corner of another building. The sha chi (or secret arrows) thus generated can be dealt with in many ways including the placement of mirrors, chimes and so on. However, it may also be feasible to arrange the shop interior at an angle, so that instead of following the four walls, the display of goods cuts across the corners. This has the further benefit of encouraging the customers to wander around the shop, in contrast to the 'four-cornered approach' (i.e. following the essentially square or rectangular shape as defined by the building) where corners can become problem areas which get cluttered and contribute to the poor flow of chi.

The result and natural response to being faced with this negative chi is to be defensive and protective which is probably not a good emotion to have when it comes to business and the job of communicating and selling. The ideal sites in figure 53 have the road aligned across the front of the building and if the door is at the corner (as indicated by the broken line) of the building, then so much the better. This idea developed from the practice mentioned above of laying out the shop interior at an angle to the building. If a building has a poor location and orientation, moving the position of the door affects the whole Feng Shui analysis, in effect, altering the position of the building itself. This arrangement was adopted a great deal, and still is, because it is generally considered that putting the doorway across the corner of a building is good Feng Shui practice. In some businesses, the door can be set at an angle and also set back allowing display windows to be placed alongside the extended entrance enabling customers to browse.

Once someone has stepped over the threshold to go inside an office building, the reception area is where most people gain their initial impression of the company. So, even if the building itself is not in an ideal location, much can be achieved inside and particularly in the entrance. Mirrors can be used to a certain extent to reflect bad chi and chimes or similar hanging items may be useful. A welcoming and positive area with good Feng Shui can be created by the use of screens, plants, and perhaps even a fountain. This can block a less than interesting view outside, which in many cases may be urban sprawl or industrial sites. This aspect also links to the five elements, because the introduction of screens and plants represents wood, a fountain or pond is water, red fish in an aquarium fire and water, and stones around the fountain or pond are earth. In this way, the moderating influences can be introduced, in unison with the layout of rooms also recommended for good Feng Shui.

Applying the five elements

Bringing together all the information regarding the five elements, this can be used to assess an office and its immediate location to try to ensure that it is best suited to the business to be carried out there. The element of the location itself must be determined by taking account of, in particular, the direction of facing, and also the surrounding area. In many cases the office will be situated in a city and therefore we should look at the surrounding buildings. Are there a lot of tower blocks, steep roofs, arched buildings, and so on? This will give an indication of the element of the location that can then be assesses against the element of the building.

When this has been established, the five elements can be studied in relation to the business activity to be undertaken and the product coming out of the business. The important factor here is to have the element that most closely matches the business activity through the element produced. That is, if wood is likely to be the best element, then water is a good element because that generates wood in the cycle. If the element of the building does not match the element required, then this is when the use of moderating elements becomes very important.

In the office

There are two basic elements to most office buildings – the offices themselves, the rooms where everyone works, and the corridors connecting them all. Many buildings layouts are now open-plan but most will have some rooms with joining corridors.

The guidelines and suggestions made about corridors with reference to the home apply equally well here (*see* section on internal doors). In essence, the points to remember are that too many doors in a corridor or hallway can lead to confusion and, ideally, doors should be placed at regular intervals. Doors should not overlap each other a little as this indicates antagonism and

Figure 54 – positioning a desk within an office; good positioning (top) and bad positioning (bottom)

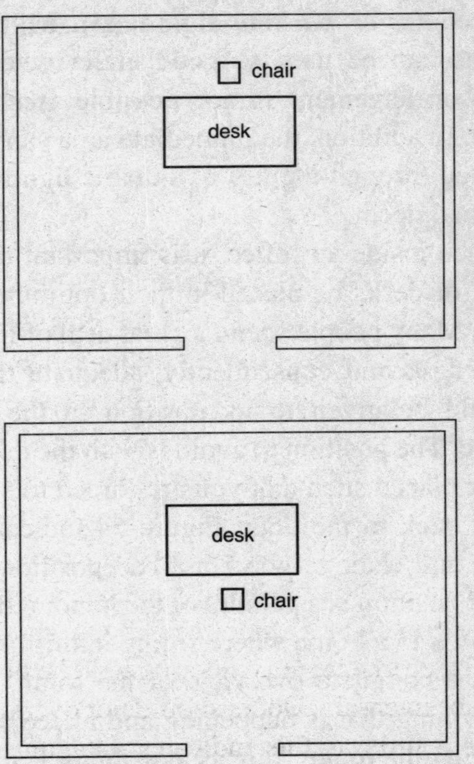

probably the best arrangement, if a number of doors are necessary, is to have them regularly spaced (*refer back to* figure 23). Mirrors or plants can be used to good effect where this ideal arrangement is not possible (*see* figure 23c). In addition, the immediate area can be improved through the use of suitable lighting and internal decor.

Once inside an office, it is important that the desk or desks be placed in their optimum position. Many people spend a great deal of time sat at a desk and consequently, adequate thought should be given to its position in the office space. The position to avoid is with the desk and chair placed such that you are forced to sit with your back to the door. Figure 54 indicates the desk and chair in good and bad positions. The good position is a parallel of the honoured-guest position in a home where sitting in this chair allows a complete overview of the room, to see everything that is happening and to see anyone entering the room. Another possibility is to place

Figure 55

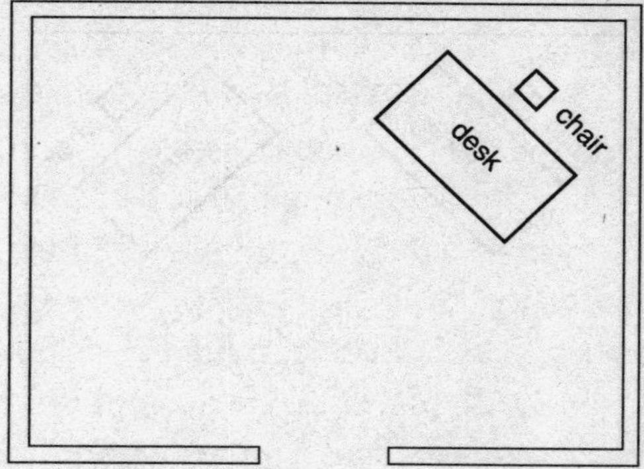

the desk diagonally across a corner of the room but still allowing full vision of the door (*see* figure 55). If there are two desks in this office, then the diagonal configuration is ideal (*see* figure 56) as it allows both occupants to have a good position with respect to the door and each other, i.e. they are not forced to sit opposite each other, in a more confrontational set up. This is an interesting development because placing the desks in this way begins to conform to the shape of the Pah Kwa.

Figure 56

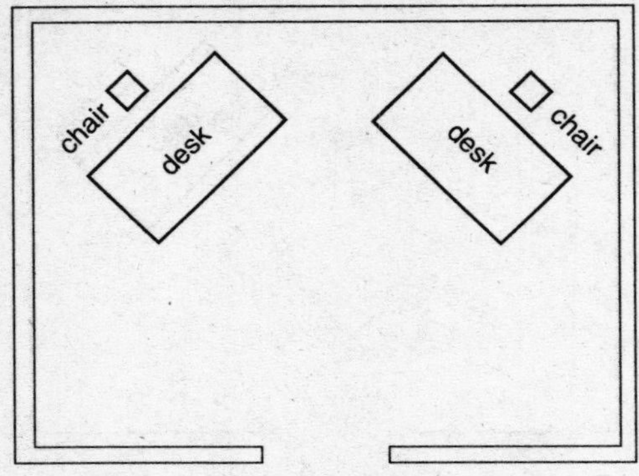

Ideally a desk should not be placed so that it is in a direct line to the door; it is important to be facing the door but at an angle, as indicated in figure 55. Also, the desk should neither face or back directly on to a window. Other options for placing the desk, other than diagonally across the top corner of the room are shown in figure 57 and in each the desk is at an angle to the door. If it is preferable for whatever reason to have the

Figure 57 – further options for placing a desk in an office

Figure 58 – remedial action to be taken if the desk is facing the door

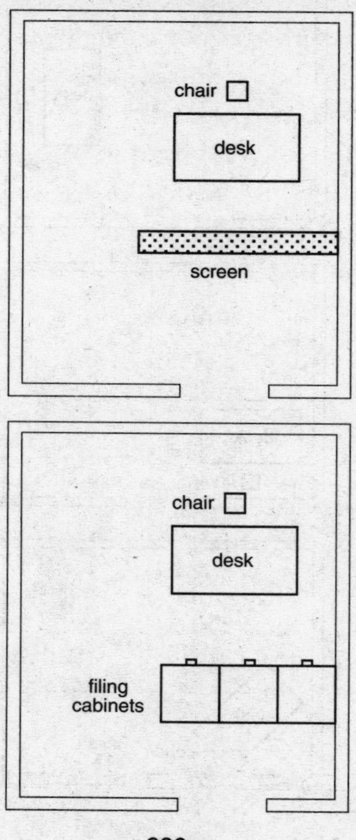

desk facing the door, then it will help if the direct line to the door can be blocked by some sort of screen or perhaps filing cabinets (*see* figure 58).

In some offices, there are a number of desks to be accommodated, whether it is the open-plan type of office or what used to be called the typing pool. In either case it is important that the arrangement of desks is such that there are as few straight lines as possible. The configuration should not create channels along which the chi

Figure 59

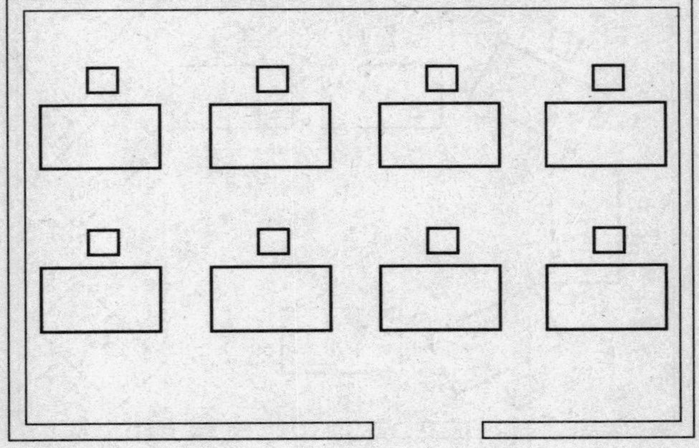

flows too quickly; in all cases remember the need to create flowing lines for the gentle circulation of chi. Figures 59 and 60 indicate the bad and good location of desks respectively, in this situation. The optimum octagonal Pah Kwa shape can be attempted as shown in figure 60, but the position of the door does hinder this somewhat. Remember also that this is only a diagrammatic representation and an office with eight desks, with associated office furniture

Figure 60

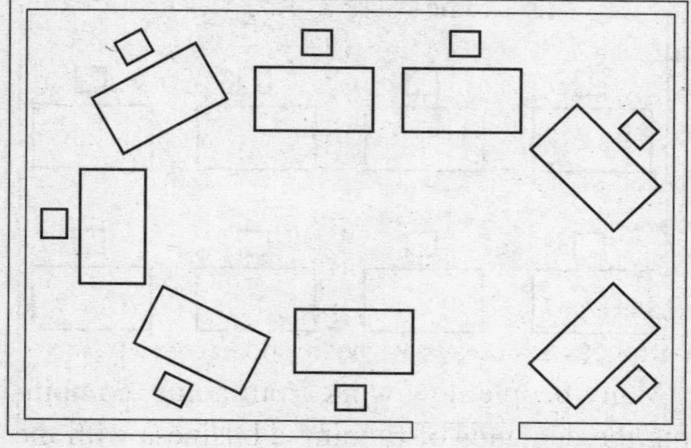

would inevitably be larger than that drawn here! However, it does indicate the sort of layout that should be attempted. If, for any reason, and particularly in an office containing a single desk, it is not possible to have a set-up where the desk faces the door, then a remedy is to place a mirror on the wall that the desk faces. At least then the occupant can see who is entering the room.

An open plan office can sometimes occupy the whole floor of a building and contain twenty or thirty desks. In this case it is not sensible or possible to configure the space as one office and therefore screens are used to create corridors and small office-like areas. The same principles apply and within each screened-off area, the desk can be paced in the best position. The use of such screens does have the added benefit of allowing plants to be trailed over corners, pictures and mirrors to be placed strategically and pathways/corridors and entrances to areas to be positioned correctly.

Many people now work from home, combining the demands of running a business with the needs of a family. It is therefore often necessary to use, as an office, a room that also doubles as, for example, a lounge. There are a number of aspects to consider which would be applied to an office but which may be affected by being in the home environment. The office should obviously be propitious to work, but at the same time be peaceful. This can often be difficult, particularly if there are other people in the room, and especially if they are children! This can to some extent be dealt with by the creation of an office space through the use of screens or, as shown above, by the strategic placing of filing cabinets or bookshelves. This shows it is a different area, with a different function and yet it is not totally cut off from everything else. The office should not be too cramped, nor need it be too roomy and a rectangular area is probably best. The feeling generated in the room should lead to clarity of thought, another good reason for partially delineating the office area in another room. If the view out of the window is not very pleasant, then curtains or plants should be placed over the window to help stop the sha chi. The centre of the room should be kept clear so the other items of office furniture – chairs, filing cabinets, bookshelves and so on – have to be placed around the edge of the room, although preferably not simply stood against the walls. The same principles apply here as elsewhere in Feng Shui, the most auspicious arrangement is that which mirrors the Pah Kwa, thus some items – for example, the bookshelves – could be placed across a corner.

When deciding upon the layout of the room, the *eight point method* can be used (*see* figure 13 and associated text). By placing the points upon the room plan, it is possible to determine the more auspicious positions for the furniture, but particularly the desk. Of course, an office is not used solely for business, commerce etc. in the strictest sense. It may also be where a designer works, or an illustrator, or an author. The position of the desk may therefore be important.

The following provides a guide:

For	Place the desk at
business, finance, commerce and related	money, eminence, wisdom, career, friends
artistic and literary pursuits	wisdom, eminence, friends
activities related to children (books, games, etc.)	children
social pursuits	marriage, friends, children, family

When the desk has been placed, then the remaining items can follow. These should be positioned carefully so that the room is tidy and uncluttered. All the items in the room – files, books and so on – should be readily accessible. The centre of the room should always be clear if at all possible and it is a good idea to place a rug at the centre. This can provide a point upon which to focus. The closer the colour of the rug is to a representation of water, the better, because deep water is considered helpful in this respect.

Procedures in Assessing the Feng Shui of a Building

Although this is certainly not an exhaustive account of Feng Shui, by bringing together all the various aspects outlined, it is now possible to survey your own office or house, or to assess a potential new home.

The first thing to decide is in which direction it faces and, whilst outside, to assess the approach in terms of roads, paths to the front door and all surroundings features both natural and man-made. These will include:

Natural

- hills and mountains
- rock slopes
- trees, whether standing alone or in groups

- water in whatever form – streams, rivers, lakes, shores, waterfalls etc.
- valleys, stream beds, fault lines

Manmade

- roads, tunnels and bridges
- railways
- canals and reservoirs
- cuttings
- electricity cables and wires, electricity pylons, gas tanks, etc.
- a variety of posts, poles and similar items
- fields, hedges and other features created in farming
- residential buildings – houses, flats, cottages, etc.
- public buildings – schools, hospitals, libraries, churches, halls, theatres and cinemas, etc.
- industrial buildings – factories, offices, warehouses, etc.
- commercial buildings – shops, markets, etc.